David P. Strauss
and Fred L. Worth

Greenwich House
Distributed by Crown Publishers, Inc.
New York

ACKNOWLEDGMENTS

The authors wish to thank the following people for their contributions and help: Ben Fernandez, Avis Meyer, Dave Glagovsky, Steve Tamerius, Vincent Terrace, David Rothel, and Ralph Albi. Special thanks to two ladies with a lot of class, Susan Worth and Vicki Ernst.

We welcome all correspondence with respect to the subject of trivia. If you have any new items or corrections to contribute toward a revised edition feel free to send them along as they will be greatly appreciated. If the authors feel your contribution is significant you will receive an acknowledgment in the next edition.

This 1984 edition is published by Greenwich House, a division of Arlington House, Inc., distributed by Crown Publishers, Inc., by arrangement with Warner Books, Inc.

Manufactured in the United States of America

Library of Congress Cataloging in Publication Data

Strauss, David P.
    Hollywood trivia.

Reprint. Originally published: New York: Warner Books, c1981.
    1. Moving-pictures—United States—Miscellanea.
I. Worth, Fred L.   II. Title.
PN1993.85.S77   1984   791.43'0973   84-12321
ISBN: 0-517-451298

h g f e d c b a

To Judy Strauss
and to Venus and Angela Worth

"The best way to become acquainted with a subject is to write a book about it."

Benjamin Disraeli

INTRODUCTION

The subtitle of this book could have been "How To Develop an Inferiority Complex." But seriously, this book is about real people, not just *reel* people. If you are surprised by the accomplishments just remember that it takes a special person to make a success of a show business career. Likewise, there are some negative items included.

Success is difficult to measure and even more difficult to predict. Who could have guessed in 1939 that Mickey Gubitosi*, just another face in *Our Gang* shorts, would some day be making in excess of $1 million a year?

---

*Robert Blake

Would anyone have thought in 1953 that a struggling actor named Charles Buchinsky*, playing Igor in *House of Wax,* would one day become the highest paid actor in the world? How could one predict in 1955 that Mary Moore**, then doing commercials as "Happy Hotpoint" on television's *Ozzie and Harriet,* would today have her own production company?

Of course for every story like those above there are literally hundreds of failures. A brief look at some of the items contained in this book will provoke many readers to wonder how anyone could possibly keep trying for stardom after years of toughing it out. Read on and discover something about your favorite star.

---

*Charles Bronson
**Mary Tyler Moore

A

Bud Abbott

In Bud Abbott's fine collection of firearms was Adolf Hitler's shotgun.

Norman Abbott, producer of the TV series *Sanford and Son,* is the nephew of comedian Bud Abbott.

Bud Abbott and Lou Costello

Bud Abbott and Lou Costello once took out a $100,000 insurance policy with Lloyds of London that stipulated payment if any of their audience should die of laughter.

Abbott and Costello were named honorary Colonels in the Wisconsin state militia.

Abbott and Costello Go to Mars

In the 1953 movie *Abbott and Costello Go to Mars*, the two comedians land on the planet Venus, not Mars.

Bud Abbott–Groucho Marx

William "Bud" Abbott and Julius "Groucho" Marx were both born on the same day—October 2, 1895.

The Absent-Minded Professor

In the 1961 Fred MacMurray movie *The Absent-Minded Professor*, Steve Allen's mother, Belle Montrose, and Keenan Wynn's son Neal both made their screen debut.

Academy Awards

Only four performers have won Academy Awards in both best and supporting acting categories. Helen Hayes received a Best Actress Award for *The Sin of Madelon Claudet* (1931/1932) and a Best Supporting Actress Award for *Airport* (1970). Ingrid Bergman won twice as Best Actress: *Gaslight* (the 1944 remake) and *Anastasia* (1956). In addition, Miss Bergman won a Best Supporting Actress Award for *Murder on the Orient Express* (1974). Maggie Smith won the Best Actress Award for *The Prime of Miss Jean Brodie* (1969) and a Best Supporting Actress Award for *California Suite* (1978). Jack Lemmon is the only male to accomplish this feat. He won a Supporting Oscar for *Mister Roberts* (1955) and was named Best Actor for *Save the Tiger* (1973).

Only two actors have been nominated for Best Actor for the same role in two different pictures. Bing Crosby achieved this in *Going My Way* (1944) and *The Bells of St. Mary's* (1945) as Father O'Malley. Peter O'Toole received the same distinction as King Henry II in *Becket* (1964) and *The Lion in Winter* (1968).

Billy Wilder took home three Oscars for his 1960 movie *The Apartment*. He won for Best Picture, Best Director, and was a co-winner for Best Story and Screenplay. Thirteen years later Marvin Hamlisch accomplished the same impressive feat for *The Sting* and *The Way We Were*. Hamlisch won for Best Song ("The Way We Were"), Best Score (*The Sting*), and Best Original Dramatic Score (*The Way We Were*). The very next year Francis Ford Coppola took home three Oscars for *The Godfather, Part II*. He won for producing, writing, and directing the movie.

In Academy Award history there have only been two ties. The first was in 1933 when the Awards for the year 1931/1932 were being made. Wallace Beery (*The Champ*) and Fredric March (*Dr. Jekyll and Mr. Hyde*) tied for Best Actor. The other occasion came in 1969 for the 1968 film season when Barbra Streisand (*Funny Girl*) and Katharine Hepburn (*The Lion in Winter*) were declared co-winners for Best Actress.

Three categories of Academy Awards were given in the first year of presentation only (1929): Best Title Writing (for silent films),

Best Artistic Quality of Production, and Best Engineering Effects.

Art Acord

Silent Western star Art Acord held the World's Championship Steer Bulldogging title in 1912. In 1916 he again won the title against Hoot Gibson.

Actresses in TV commercials

The woman who plays Mrs. Olson in the Folger's commercials is former B-movie actress Virginia Christine. The spokeswoman for Comet, Josephine, is former child star Jane Withers. Margaret Hamilton (the Wicked Witch in *The Wizard of Oz*) played Cora in Maxwell House Coffee commercials. Vivian Vance (TV's Ethel Mertz) played Maxine who sold instant coffee for Maxwell House.

Neile Adams

Actress Neile Adams, Steve McQueen's first wife, was incarcerated by the Japanese for eighteen months in the Philippines during World War II.

Nick Adams

Nick Adams had the unusual but fortunate opportunity to have been close with two legends, James Dean and Elvis Presley.

Nick Adams dubbed his voice for James Dean's in one uncompleted scene from the

1956 movie *Giant* after Dean had been killed in a car accident on September 30, 1955.

Dawn Addams

Actress Dawn Addams, who appeared in such films as *The Robe* (1953) and *Singin' in the Rain* (1952), gave up her career to marry Prince Don Vittorio Massimo of Italy.

The Adventures of Robin Hood

In 1938 James Cagney was set to play the title role in *The Adventures of Robin Hood* but he walked off the Warner Bros. lot in a dispute. *Captain Blood* was a recent hit and Errol Flynn got the part of Robin Hood. By the way, Eugene Pallette was not the first choice for the part of Friar Tuck. The original selection was Guy Kibbee.

The African Queen

There was once talk of a British production of *The African Queen* which would have starred John Mills and Bette Davis before the 1951 version with Humphrey Bogart and Katharine Hepburn.

At one time there were plans to remake *The African Queen* as a musical with Lee Marvin and Doris Day.

John Agar–Shirley Temple

When John Agar and his bride, Shirley Temple, registered at a hotel during their honeymoon they sought anonymity by signing as Emil and Emma Glutz.

Eddie Albert

At one time, Eddie Albert served as a flyer in a trapeze act.

During World War II, Eddie Albert was a civilian informant for U.S. Army Intelligence regarding activities in Mexico.

Wally Albright

Our Gang member Wally Albright won the Men's National Track and Ski Championship in 1957.

Alan Alda

Alan Alda is the son of Joan Brown (ex-Miss New York) and actor/singer Robert Alda.

At the age of ten Alan Alda was stricken with polio which paralyzed his legs for several months.

Alfie

The 1966 film *Alfie* had been turned down by Terence Stamp, Anthony Newley, and Laurence Harvey before it was offered to Michael Caine, who accepted the part and became an overnight star. Although the song "Alfie" became a big hit for Dionne Warwick it was sung by Cher in the film.

Gracie Allen

Mystery writer S.S. Van Dine (William Wright), creator of detective Philo Vance, wrote a story especially for Gracie Allen, which was made into a 1939 movie that starred her. It was titled *The Gracie Allen Murder Case*.

Woody Allen

Every Monday evening Woody Allen plays clarinet at a Manhattan night spot called Michael's Pub. Rather than let down his fellow musicians, Allen was there the evening he was awarded three Oscars for Best Picture, Best Director, and Best Screenwriter (with Marshall Brickman) for the 1977 movie *Annie Hall*.

Woody Allen–Erich Segal

Woody Allen and author Erich Segal attended the same Brooklyn high school, Midwood High.

All Quiet on the Western Front

At the conclusion of *All Quiet on the Western Front* (1930) director Lewis Milestone's hand was used for the close-up of Paul Baumer (Lew Ayres) reaching for the butterfly prior to the sniper killing Baumer.

All the King's Men

Harry Cohn, who was head of Columbia Pictures, wanted Spencer Tracy to play Willie

Stark in the 1949 movie *All the King's Men.*
Broderick Crawford eventually got the role
and won the Best Actor Award for his portrayal.

June Allyson

In her youth actress June Allyson won a
greater New York City freestyle swimming
championship. What made this remarkable is
the fact that for several years prior to this she
was forced to wear a corrective back brace due
to an injury at the age of eight.

At her 1939 graduation ceremonies from
Theodore Roosevelt High School in the Bronx
June Allyson received an award for the highest
scholastic record that year with an average of
97.3 (In comparison Barbra Streisand graduated from Erasmus High in New York with an
average of 93.)

Robert Altman

Director Robert Altman was a bomber pilot who flew forty-six missions over Borneo and
the Dutch East Indies during World War II.

Robert Altman sometimes gives characters
in his movies the names of people he actually
knows.

Eric Ambler

English novelist and screenwriter Eric Am-
bler created the television series *Checkmate.*

Don Ameche

Don Ameche was not the only person to portray Alexander Graham Bell in movies, though he did in *The Story of Alexander Graham Bell* (1939). In the 1957 movie *The Story of Mankind* Bell was portrayed by Jim Ameche, Don's brother. The brothers also appeared together in the radio program *Jack Armstrong, All-American Boy*. Jim played the title role and Don played Captain Hughes.

Cleveland Amory

Noted critic Cleveland Amory created the short-lived 1965 series *O. K. Crackerby*, which starred Burl Ives.

Eddie Anderson

Eddie "Rochester" Anderson's mother, Ella Mae, had been a circus tightrope walker in her youth.

Ursula Andress

Rolf Andress, father of actress Ursula Andress, was a Swiss diplomat.

Dana Andrews–Steve Forrest

Dana Andrews and his actor brother Steve Forrest (two of eight brothers) were born the sons of a Baptist minister in Don't, Mississippi. The family name is Andrews.

Stanley Andrews

Television's Old Ranger from the series *Death Valley Days,* Stanley Andrews, was the radio voice of Daddy Warbucks on *Little Orphan Annie.*

Anna and the King of Siam

Producer Darryl F. Zanuck's first choices for the role of the King in *Anna and the King of Siam* (1946) were James Mason and Robert Montgomery. The part went to Rex Harrison, his first American film.

Anne of the Thousand Days

In the 1969 movie *Anne of the Thousand Days* which starred Richard Burton and Genevieve Bujold, Elizabeth Taylor appeared as an unbilled extra in one scene as a reveler. She had also appeared in a crowd scene, again unbilled, in the 1951 movie *Quo Vadis?*.

Annie Get Your Gun

Betty Hutton took over for an ailing Judy Garland in the 1950 movie *Annie Get Your Gun.* In the same movie Louis Calhern replaced Frank Morgan who had died.

Fatty Arbuckle

Roscoe "Fatty" Arbuckle weighed sixteen pounds at birth.

Fatty Arbuckle was the first actor to give a cigarette endorsement. It was for Murads.

After the notorious Fatty Arbuckle scandal of the early 1920's, Arbuckle went on to direct a few films under the name William Goodrich. Buster Keaton suggested he use Will B. Good.

Alan Arkin

In 1956 a calypso group called The Terriers had a hit song on Glory Records titled "The Banana Boat Song." One of the members of the group was future actor Alan Arkin.

Richard Arlen

Richard Arlen, star of *Wings* (1927), had been a member of the Royal Canadian Flying Corps during World War I, but saw no action.

Armed and Extremely Dangerous

In 1978 the Soviet Union finally filmed their first Western movie, titled *Armed and Extremely Dangerous*.

Desi Arnaz

Desi Arnaz's father and great-grandfather were both mayors of Santiago, Cuba. His father served as the city's youngest mayor at age twenty-nine. His grandfather Don Desiderio was a doctor with Teddy Roosevelt's Rough Riders.

James Arness

Actor James Arness was wounded in the leg while landing with the U.S. Army at Anzio in 1944.

James Arness–Montgomery Clift

James Arness and Montgomery Clift both had twin sisters.

Dorothy Arnold

Marilyn Monroe wasn't the first actress to marry baseball great Joe DiMaggio. Joltin' Joe met his first wife, Dorothy Arnold, when the two appeared together in the 1937 movie *Manhattan Merry-Go-Round*.

Edward Arnold

Movie heavyweight Edward Arnold once seriously considered running for the U.S. Senate representing California.

Around the World in Eighty Days

The word cameo, as applied to a guest shot, was coined by Michael Todd in the making of his 1956 movie *Around the World in Eighty Days* in which he had forty-two cameo appearances by well-known actors and actresses.

Around the World in Eighty Days holds many distinctions, one of which being the movie to use the most animals: 3,800 sheep; 2,448 buffalo; 950 donkeys; 800 horses; 512 monkeys; 17 bulls; 15 elephants; 6 skunks; and 4 ostriches.

Cliff Arquette

In 1959 comedian Cliff Arquette opened a Civil War museum in Gettysburg, Pennsylvania.

Arsenic and Old Lace

Cary Grant gave his entire salary of $100,000 from the 1944 movie *Arsenic and Old Lace* to the U.S. War Relief.

Jean Arthur

After retiring from films, Jean Arthur taught drama at Vassar.

Anthony Asquith

English director Anthony Asquith, who directed such movies as *The VIPs* (1963) and *The Yellow Rolls Royce* (1964), was the son of the Earl of Oxford and Asquith, who once served as prime minister of Great Britain.

Fred Astaire

Fred Astaire danced so much in the making of the 1942 movie *Holiday Inn* that he lost fourteen pounds, weighing 126 pounds at the movie's completion.

Fred Astaire—Gene Kelly

Fred Astaire and Gene Kelly only danced together in one routine, titled "The Babbitt and the Bromide" in the 1946 movie *Ziegfeld Follies*. (However they did appear together in *That's Entertainment Part II* in several dance routines throughout that 1976 movie.)

Mary Astor

Mary Astor, whose real name is Lucile Langhanke, was the winner of a beauty contest sponsored by *Motion Picture* magazine when Mary was but eleven years old.

Mary Astor became the sister-in-law of director Howard Hawks when she married his brother Kenneth in 1928. They were divorced in 1930.

After her retirement from films Mary Astor turned to the world of writing and conquered that one too with several successful books. Both her 1959 and 1967 autobiographies, *My Story* and *A Life on Film,* sold well. She even attempted the world of fiction in 1961 with *The Incredible Charlie Careue* and again in the same year with *Baby Kate*. She has also authored a children's book titled *My Friends Have Blue Eyes*.

Lionel Atwill

Lionel Atwill was to have been the star of the 3-D classic *House of Wax* (1953) but died before the project was started, and the part went to Vincent Price.

Gene Autry

Gene Autry, the composer of over 275 songs, once worked as a telegrapher for the Frisco railroad in Oklahoma.

Several other cowboys sang before Gene Autry made a fortune doing it. They included Warner Baxter, Ken Maynard, Bob Steele, and John Wayne, whose singing was actually done by Smith Ballew in the *Singin' Sandy* series.

In November, 1941, the town of Berwyn, Oklahoma, changed its name to Gene Autry, Oklahoma.

During World War II Gene Autry served as an Army Air Corps pilot flying the China–Burma–India Theater of Operations.

Gene Autry actually has an estate called Melody Ranch in the San Fernando Valley.

Lew Ayres

Lew Ayres played with several orchestras (such as those of Henry Halstead and Ray West) prior to becoming an actor.

During World War II Lew Ayres served in a labor camp as a conscientious objector. His stand on the war cost him many film roles, and his career suffered for years.

B

Baa Baa Black Sheep

Dirk Blocker, the son of late actor Dan Blocker, and James Whitmore Jr., appeared together in the first season of the TV series *Baa Baa Black Sheep* (*Black Sheep Squadron* in its second season).

Lauren Bacall

Lauren Bacall's mother, Natalie Weinstein, changed her name to Bacal, which means wine glass in Rumanian, the same as Weinstein in German. (Lauren, born Betty Joan Perske, added the second "l" to Bacal.)

When she was a teenager in New York Lauren Bacall worked as an usherette at theaters like the Morosco, the Golden, and the St. James. She modeled for Montgomery Ward catalogues, and in 1942 she was crowned Miss Greenwich Village.

Lauren Bacall was discovered by producer Howard Hawks's wife, when she appeared on the cover of *Harper's Bazaar* magazine.

Susan Backlinie

Actress Susan Backlinie played the first victim in both the 1975 movie *Jaws* and the 1977 movie *Grizzly*.

Jim Backus

Jim Backus, the voice of Mr. Magoo, had a novelty record in 1958 titled "Delicious" that entered the national charts. It was a cut from his album *Dirty Old Man.*

The Bad and the Beautiful

The 1952 movie *The Bad and the Beautiful* was originally to have been called *Tribute to a Bad Man* with Clark Gable as the lead. Kirk Douglas eventually got the part. However, the discarded title was used four years later for a James Cagney film.

Barbara Bain

Prior to her acting career Barbara Bain modeled for *Vogue* and other magazines.

Fay Bainter

Academy Award-winning actress Fay Bainter is buried in Arlington National Cemetery with her husband, Lt. Commander Reginald Venable.

Carroll Baker

In 1964 an African Masai chieftain was so fascinated by blonde actress Carroll Baker that he offered 150 cows, 200 goats and sheep, and $750 for her while she was on location for the 1965 movie *Mister Moses*.

Lucille Ball

Lucille Ball once registered as a voter for the Communist party as a favor to her grandfather.

One of Lucille Ball's early breaks came when she was selected as the model for a billboard depicting the Chesterfield Cigarette Girl.

Lucille Ball and her son Desi Arnaz IV appeared on the first cover of *TV Guide* magazine in 1953.

Lucille Ball became the first woman to receive the Friars Club Life Achievement Award for her numerous contributions to the field of entertainment.

Lucille Ball–Desi Arnaz

My Favorite Husband was the radio program that inspired *I Love Lucy*. It starred Lucille Ball and Richard Denning as Liz and

George Cooper. The program was based on a book titled *Mr. and Mrs. Cugat*. Coincidentally, Desi Arnaz worked for a time with the Xavier Cugat orchestra.

Martin Balsam

Actor Martin Balsam became Dick Van Patten's brother-in-law when he married Van Patten's sister Joyce in 1957. They were divorced in 1962.

Clara Blandick

May Robson and Janet Beecher were considered for the role of Auntie Em in *The Wizard of Oz* (1939) that went to Clara Blandick.

Tallulah Bankhead

Tallulah Bankhead's father was William Bankhead (Dem.—Alabama), Speaker of the House of Representatives. William's brother, John, was a U.S. senator who served for twelve years. Her grandfather John was also a member of the Senate.

At age fifteen Tallulah Bankhead won first place in a contest sponsored by *Photoplay* magazine. They ran her entry as the Girl of Mystery because she forgot to include her name. Five other girls claimed the picture as their own. When it was discovered who the mystery girl was, Tallulah received her prize, a trip to Hollywood.

Tallulah Bankhead and Alice Roosevelt, daughter of President Theodore Roosevelt, were schoolmates and friends at Fairmont Seminary in Washington, D.C.

Proctor & Gamble once put out a hair shampoo named Tallulah. Miss Bankhead sued successfully over their unauthorized use of her name.

President Harry S Truman once claimed that Tallulah Bankhead's 1952 autobiography was the best book he had read since coming to the White House.

At one time Tallulah Bankhead owned a pet lion named Winston.

Tallulah Bankhead was the first white woman to appear on the cover of *Ebony* magazine.

Vilma Banky

Actress Vilma Banky, one-time wife of Rod La Rocque, once won the golf championship at the Wilshire Country Club in Los Angeles.

John Banner–Robert Clary

John Banner, who played the apathetic German Sergeant Hans Schultz in the TV series *Hogan's Heroes,* once posed for U.S. Army recruiting posters. Robert Clary, who played Louis LeBeau on the same series, actually spent three years in German concentration camps during World War II. On his left forearm is the tattoo A5714.

Jim Bannon

Prior to becoming an actor (playing Red Ryder in films), Jim Bannon was a sportscaster.

Theda Bara

It has often been stated that Theda Bara's name was an anagram of arab death. Such publicity was common in Miss Bara's days. Actually her name comes from a shortening of her own true first name, Theodosia, and her grandfather's name, Barranger.

Brigitte Bardot

At the age of thirteen Brigitte Bardot won an excellency award from the Paris Conservatory in ballet. She has performed ballet on French television.

Baretta

Jack Oakie, Burgess Meredith, and Joe Campanella were all considered for the part of Baretta's (Robert Blake) pal, Billy Truman, on the TV series *Baretta*. The part went to Tom Ewell.

Lex Barker

Movie Tarzan Lex Barker was a descendant of Roger Williams, founder of Rhode Island colony.

The Barkleys of Broadway

The Barkleys of Broadway (1949) was planned for Judy Garland. When she became ill, Ginger Rogers received the role.

Sydney S. Barlett

Film writer and producer Sydney S. Barlett (*Twelve O'clock High* and *A Gathering of Eagles*) was the first American officer to participate in a bombing raid on Berlin with the RAF in March 1943.

Rona Barrett

At the age of thirteen Rona Barrett was the nationwide coordinator of the Eddie Fisher Fan Clubs.

Wendy Barrie

Wendy Barrie's grandfather, General Sir Charles Warren, was once the head of Scotland Yard. Her godfather, Sir James Barrie, was the author of *Peter Pan*.

Wendy Barrie was once engaged to gangster Benjamin "Bugsy" Siegel.

Chuck Barris

Chuck Barris, who created TV programs like *The Dating Game*, *The Newlywed Game*, and *The Gong Show*, wrote "Palisades Park," a hit record by Freddie Cannon in 1962.

Gene Barry

Actor Gene Barry (TV's Bat Masterson) was once the vocalist for Teddy Powell's band.

John Barrymore—Thelma Ritter

John Barrymore and Thelma Ritter were both born on Valentine's Day, 1882 and 1905 respectively.

Lionel Barrymore

Lionel Barrymore once authored a novel titled *Mr. Cantonwine: A Moral Tale.*

Some of Lionel Barrymore's musical compositions have been performed by the Philadelphia and San Francisco symphony orchestras.

Freddie Bartholomew

Former child-star Freddie Bartholomew is today the producer of the television soap *As the World Turns.*

Freddie Bartholomew—Marcello Mastroianni

Freddie Bartholomew and Marcello Mastroianni share the same birthday, September 28, 1924.

Baseball

Gene Autry is part-owner of the California Angels. Bing Crosby was part-owner of the

Pittsburgh Pirates. Bob Hope is part-owner of the Cleveland Indians, and Danny Kaye is an owner of the Seattle Mariners.

James Baskett

Sidney Poitier was not the first black man to receive an Oscar. James Baskett, who played Uncle Remus in *Song of the South* (1946), received a Special Academy Award.

Florence Bates

Actress Florence Bates became the first woman lawyer in Texas in 1914 at the age of twenty-six.

Anne Baxter

Anne Baxter's grandfather was architect Frank Lloyd Wright.

Warner Baxter

Warner Baxter got the part of the Cisco Kid for the movie *In Old Arizona* (1929) by accident. Veteran director Raoul Walsh was set to play the romantic hero until a startled jackrabbit crashed through the windshield of a jeep he was driving and blinded his right eye. Baxter, star of many Westerns, had a fear of horses.

Matthew Beard

Matthew Beard, better known as *Our Gang* member Stymie, spent six years in prison for pushing drugs.

Beat the Clock

James Dean and Warren Oates both tested stunts for the TV game show *Beat the Clock* prior to achieving success as actors.

Warren Beatty

Actor Warren Beatty is the younger brother of actress Shirley MacLaine. Their real last name is Beaty.

At Washington and Lee High School in Arlington, Virginia, Warren Beatty, who was president of his class, was a star center on the football team. When he was graduated, he received ten offers of football scholarships. He turned them all down.

Warren Beatty rejected the male lead in the following motion pictures: *The Sting* (1973), *The Way We Were* (1973), and *The Great Gatsby* (1974). All three were then done by Robert Redford.

Warren Beatty–Ryan O'Neal

Warren Beatty and Ryan O'Neal both played supporting parts on the TV series *The Many Loves of Dobie Gillis*.

Beauty contests

Many show-business personalities arrived in Hollywood via beauty contests. To wit:

Runners-up in the Miss America Pageant:
Jeanne Crain, 1941

Cloris Leachman, 1947
Vera Miles, 1948
Anita Bryant, 1958
Winners of the Miss America title:
Rosemary La Planche, 1941
Bess Myerson, 1945
Lee Meriwether, 1955
Mary Ann Mobley, 1959

Becky Sharp

Becky Sharp, a 1935 movie starring Miriam Hopkins, was the first full-length movie filmed in color.

Thelma Catherine Ryan (Mrs. Pat Nixon) had a walk-on part in *Becky Sharp*, but the scene ended up on the cutting-room floor.

Wallace Beery

Actor Wallace Beery was once an elephant trainer with the Ringling Brothers Circus.

Wallace Beery made his movie debut as a Swedish servant *girl* in the 1914 film *Swedie*.

For thirty-five years Wallace Beery held the world's record for the largest black sea bass which he caught off Catalina Island in 1916. His prize weighed in at 515 pounds.

Harry Belafonte

In the 1954 movie *Carmen Jones* the great calypso/folk singer Harry Belafonte had his singing voice dubbed by LaVern Hutcherson.

Rex Bell

Actor Rex Bell, husband of "*It* Girl" Clara Bow, was elected to two terms as the Lt.-Governor of Nevada.

Ralph Bellamy

Ralph Bellamy is a descendant of author Edward Bellamy, who wrote the utopian novel *Looking Backward* in 1887.

Peter Benchley

Peter Benchley, whose two novels *Jaws* and *The Deep* were made into movies (1975 and 1977) is a former speech writer for President Lyndon B. Johnson.

Peter Benchley, son of novelist Nathaniel Benchley and grandson of humorist Robert Benchley, made cameo appearances in both of the films based on his books. In *Jaws* he was a reporter, and in *The Deep* he played the first mate who had served aboard the ship *Goliath*.

William Bendix

William Bendix's father, Max, was a conductor for the Metropolitan Opera in New York City.

William Bendix, who portrayed Babe Ruth in the 1948 movie *The Babe Ruth Story*, was actually a bat boy for the New York Giants and the New York Yankees in his youth. Bendix also played two summers of semi-pro baseball as a second baseman.

William Bendix–Robert Taylor–Clark Gable

William Bendix played a cabdriver in seven movies. Robert Taylor, whose father was a doctor, played a doctor in five films. Clark Gable played a newsman in nine films.

Beneath the Planet of the Apes

The underground New York sets used in the 1970 film *Beneath the Planet of the Apes* were originally built for the 1969 film *Hello Dolly!*

Ben Hur

In the 1925 silent version of *Ben Hur* the stuntmen were offered a $150 bonus for the man who won the chariot race, $100 for second place, and $50 for third. This was done to increase the enthusiasm of the stuntmen, which it did.

Both Cesare Danova and Rock Hudson were considered for the title role of the 1959 remake of *Ben Hur*, while Charlton Heston was slated to play Messala. Instead, Heston played the title role.

In the 1959 version of *Ben Hur* both Charlton Heston and Stephen Boyd, who played Messala, had blue eyes. Stephen Boyd had to wear dark contact lenses so his eyes would photograph another color for the film. Only Charlton Heston's blue eyes sparkled.

Bruce Bennett

Movie Tarzan Bruce Bennett (born Herman Brix) won a Silver Medal in the shot put competition at the 1928 Olympics held in Amsterdam.

Constance Bennett

Constance Bennett, who died on July 24, 1965, was buried at Arlington National Cemetery. Her husband, Brigadier General John Coulter, was a commander of McGuire Air Force Base.

Jack Benny

Jack Benny once appeared on the TV quiz program *The $64,000 Question*. After answering the first question correctly Benny quit and took home $64.00. His category was violins.

Jack Benny had a junior high school named after him in his hometown of Waukegan, Illinois. The school football team is called the 39ers.

John Beradino

John Beradino, who plays Dr. Steve Hardy on the TV soap opera *General Hospital*, played baseball for the old St. Louis Browns. In 1948 he played with the Cleveland Indians who won the World Series that year.

Edgar Bergen–Jimmy Nelson

Ventriloquists Edgar Bergen and Jimmy Nelson both attended the same Chicago school, Lake View High.

Ingrid Bergman

Ingrid Bergman and her husband, director Roberto Rossellini, are the parents of twin girls, both of whom are beginning careers in films.

Milton Berle

Milton Berle made his screen debut as a baby being thrown from a train in an episode of the 1914 serial *The Perils of Pauline*.

Milton Berle, dubbed the "Thief of Bad Gags," was actually taken to court in 1936 by two other comedians who accused Berle of stealing their material. Berle, who owns a card file of thousands upon thousands of jokes dating back over a hundred years, won the case.

Milton Berle was the first *man* to make the list of the worst-dressed women of the year. Singer David Bowie was the second.

Berle claims to have lost over $3.5 million in gambling.

Milton Berle–Bob Hope

In their youth both Milton Berle and Bob Hope won prizes in Charlie Chaplin imitation contests.

Irving Berlin–Eddie Cantor

Israel Baline is Irving Berlin's real name. Edward Israel Itskowitz was Eddie Cantor's real name.

Herschel Bernardi

Herschel Bernardi, who spent three years as Lieutenant Jacobi on TV's *Peter Gunn,* is the voice of the Jolly Green Giant and of Charlie the Tuna.

Sarah Bernhardt

Sarah Bernhardt was supposedly the first woman to wear pants as regular feminine apparel.

French stage actress Sarah Bernhardt, who was portrayed in the 1976 movie *The Incredible Sarah* by Glenda Jackson, occasionally slept in a coffin.

Ken Berry

Comic and dancer Ken Berry was once a singer with Horace Heidt's band.

Best Foot Forward

Lucille Ball got a part in the 1943 movie *Best Foot Forward* when Lana Turner became pregnant with her daughter Cheryl.

The Best Years of Our Lives

Fredric March replaced William Powell in the 1946 movie *The Best Years of Our Lives.* March won an Oscar for the role.

Betrayed

Clark Gable's last movie for MGM was also the only one for which the studio refused to increase Gable's salary. The 1954 movie was by chance named *Betrayed*.

Beulah

The role of Beulah the maid, originating on the radio program *Fibber McGee and Molly*, was first played by a white male, Marlin Hurt.

Charles Bickford

Charles Bickford was once a sparring partner for heavyweight boxer Jim Corbett.

The Big City

Jim Thorpe, James J. Jeffries, and Jack Dempsey all made bit appearances in the 1937 Spencer Tracy film *The Big City*.

The Big Mouth

Chicken magnate Colonel Harlan T. Sanders made a cameo appearance in the 1967 Jerry Lewis movie *The Big Mouth*.

The Big Steal

Robert Mitchum asked for a delay in his sentencing on a marijuana possession charge in 1949 in order to complete filming of *The Big Steal*.

The Big Valley

During the first year of production on the TV series *The Big Valley* Lee (Six Million

Dollar Man) Majors was paid only about $20,000. This amounted to less than what was spent on Barbara Stanwyck's wardrobe.

Theodore Bikel

Actor Theodore Bikel claims he speaks seventeen different languages, ranging from Greek to Zulu.

The Birth of a Nation

The first film shown in the White House was *The Birth of a Nation* (1915), when Woodrow Wilson was President.

Joey Bishop

Comedian Joey Bishop was the smallest baby ever born at Fordham Hospital in New York City. His weight was 2 pounds, 14 ounces.

Joey Bishop received a citation from Pope John XXIII for his help with the Boys' Towns throughout Italy.

Julie Bishop

The mother of actress Julie Bishop has been married to both General Douglas MacArthur and actor Lionel Atwill.

Karen Black–Genevieve Bujold

Actresses Karen Black and Geneviève Bujold were both born on July 1, 1942.

Janet Blair

Strawberry blonde actress Janet Blair once sang with Hal Kemp's orchestra. She married the band's pianist, Lou Busch.

Marie Blake

Marie Blake, who played Sally the switchboard operator in the *Dr. Kildare* movie series, and who later appeared on the TV series *The Addams Family* (under the stage name Blossom Rock) as the grandmother, was really named Edith MacDonald, the younger sister of actress Jeanette MacDonald.

Robert Blake

If his temperament had not conflicted with that of Barbra Streisand, Robert Blake would have played Fanny Brice's husband, Billy Rose, in the movie *Funny Lady* (1975). He was replaced by James Caan.

Mel Blanc

Mel Blanc, the voice of Bugs Bunny, is allergic to carrots.

Sally Blane

Actress Sally Blane is the sister of Loretta Young and the wife of director Norman Foster.

The Blob

Steve McQueen received only $3,000 for his starring role in the 1958 movie *The Blob*.

Joan Blondell

Ed Blondell, the father of actresses Joan and Gloria Blondell, was the original Katzenjammer Kid on the vaudeville stage.

Joan Blondell, a former Miss Dallas, was the author of the best-selling 1972 novel *Center Door Fancy*.

Ann Blyth

At the age of nine Ann Blyth was a member of the New York Children's Opera Company.

In 1953 Ann Blyth married Dr. James McNulty, the brother of singer Dennis Day, in a ceremony in which Pope Pius XII gave a special benediction.

Dirk Bogarde

British actor Dirk Bogarde's father was the art editor for the *London Times*. Two of Bogarde's sketches of the D-Day invasion, in which he took part, are on display at the British War Museum.

In the 1977 war film *A Bridge Too Far*, Dirk Bogarde portrayed Lt. General Frederick Browning. Bogarde had actually been involved in the battle for Arnhem Bridge in September,

1944, as a captain under Browning, the man he portrayed.

Humphrey Bogart

According to biographer Nathaniel Benchley, Humphrey Bogart received his scarred lip as a result of being smashed in the mouth by the manacled wrists of an Allied prisoner he was transporting during World War I. Bogey dropped the man with one shot from his .45 automatic.

Humphrey Bogart's coffin had a small gold whistle placed in it by his wife, Lauren Bacall.

Humphrey Bogart–Lauren Bacall

Humphrey Bogart was suspended eleven times from Warner Bros. for refusing roles, and Lauren Bacall was suspended twelve times from the same studio for the same reason.

Humphrey Bogart–Charles Bronson

Humphrey Bogart and Charles Bronson both made their screen debuts at age thirty-one, the same age at which Rudolph Valentino's career prematurely ended.

Humphrey Bogart–James Cagney

Warner Bros. changed the birthdates of two of its major stars. Bogart's was changed from January 23, 1899 to December 25, 1900.

Cagney's was changed from July 14, 1899, to July 14, 1904.

Humphrey Bogart–Katharine Hepburn

Humphrey Bogart and Katharine Hepburn, who were both nominated for Oscars in their only film together, *The African Queen* (1951), each had fathers who were doctors.

Bojangles

Bill "Bojangles" Robinson met his manager Marty Forkins when, while a waiter, he spilled a bowl of oyster stew on Forkins's lap. He convinced his future manager that he was not a waiter but a dancer. Once Forkins saw him dance he elected to become his manager.

Bill Robinson, best known for dancing, also held three records for running races backwards. He ran the 50-yard dash in 6.0 seconds, the 75-yard dash in 8.2 seconds, and the 100-yard dash in only 13.2 seconds.

The slang word "copacetic" was coined by dancer Bill "Bojangles" Robinson.

John Boles

During World War I, actor John Boles worked for American espionage services and was present at the Paris Peace Conference attended by President Wilson, General John Pershing, and French President Raymond Poincaré.

John Boles had a few hit records such as

"It Happened in Monterey" and "You, You Alone."

Ray Bolger–George Raft–Ruby Keeler

Dancers Ray Bolger, George Raft, and Ruby Keeler were all raised on the same Tenth Avenue block in New York City.

James Bond

James Mason, Trevor Howard, Peter Finch, and Richard Burton were among those considered for the part of James Bond.

Of the five actors who have played James Bond, only one (Roger Moore) is British by birth. Barry Nelson is American, Sean Connery and David Niven are Scottish, and George Lazenby is Australian.

Tommy Bond

Tommy Bond, who played the tough kid, "Butch," in the *Our Gang* series, married Miss California of 1943, Polly Ellis.

Ward Bond

Actor Ward Bond served as John Wayne's best man when Wayne married Esperanza Baur. On his way to the church Bond was hit by a car; he performed his duty at the ceremony on crutches. John Wayne was later best man at Bond's wedding.

Beulah Bondi

Beulah Bondi was first announced for the part of Ma Joad in the 1940 movie *The Grapes of Wrath*. The role went to Jane Darwell who won the Best Supporting Actress Award for her performance.

Bongo

Bongo, the unicycling bear in Walt Disney cartoons, was created by Pulitzer Prize-winning author Sinclair Lewis.

Pat Boone

In high school Pat Boone worked on the school paper, was a member of the baseball, basketball, and track teams, and was president of the student body. He was also voted "most popular boy." Singer Roy Orbison was a classmate of Boone's at North Texas State College.

Pat Boone is the son-in-law of the late great member of the Country Music Hall of Fame, Red Foley. Boone is also part-owner of the Golden State Warriors basketball team.

Ernest Borgnine

Ernest Borgnine, star of television's *McHale's Navy*, spent ten years in the U.S. Navy prior to becoming an actor.

Hobart Bosworth

Character actor Hobart Bosworth claimed to be a descendant of Miles Standish.

Clara Bow

In 1921 sixteen-year-old Clara Bow won a screen test sponsored by *Motion Picture Classic* magazine.

Clara Bow–Thelma Todd

Clara Bow and Thelma Todd were both born on July 29, 1905.

Major Bowes

Major Edward Bowes of radio's *Original Amateur Hour* had been a major in Army intelligence during World War I.

Stephen Boyd

At the age of sixteen Stephen Boyd made his acting debut on stage in Ulster, Ireland, playing the role of a sixty-year-old man.

Stephen Boyd–Gina Lollobrigida

Stephen Boyd and Gina Lollobrigida were both born on July 4, 1928. Boyd was born in Belfast, Ireland, and Lollobrigida in Subiaco, Italy.

William Boyd

William Boyd, who later would be identified on radio, in movies, and on television as Hopalong Cassidy, had his career nearly ruined in the early 1930s when his studio cancelled his contract after a Broadway actor, also named William Boyd, was arrested on various charges. The newspapers showed the photo of the future Hopalong, thus associating the wrong actor to the other's misdeeds. Although Boyd was completely innocent, it wasn't until he was billed as Hopalong Cassidy that his career turned around.

William Boyd's hair turned white when he was only twenty-one years old, giving him the distinct look for which he was famous.

Charles Boyer

French-born Charles Boyer established the French Research Foundation.

Boy Meets Girl

Ole Olsen and Chic Johnson were the first choices to play the song writers in the 1938 film *Boy Meets Girl*. The studio chose James Cagney and Pat O'Brien.

Boys' Town

Spencer Tracy gave his second Oscar for Best Actor in *Boys' Town* (1938) to Father Edward J. Flanagan, the person he had portrayed. It is now on exhibit at Boys' Town near Omaha, Nebraska. Tracy had also won an Oscar the year before for his role of Manuel in *Captains Courageous*.

Pat Brady

Pat Brady, Roy Rogers's sidekick, served in France during World War II and was awarded two Purple Hearts.

Scott Brady

Scott Brady, born Gerald Tierney (brother of actor Lawrence Tierney), was a boxing champ at Pensacola, Florida, while he was in the Navy, boxing in the light-heavyweight division. In his second film, *In This Corner* (1948), he played an ex-Navy boxer.

Neville Brand

Actor Neville Brand was the fourth highest-decorated U.S. soldier in World War II. Audie Murphy, of course, was first.

Neville Brand–John Carradine

On December 8, 1978, Neville Brand was rescued from his burning Malibu house. On the very next day actor John Carradine was rescued by firemen from his burning Oxnard apartment.

Marlon Brando

Marlon Brando's second wife was Movita Castenada, who played the Tahitian lover of Fletcher Christian (Clark Gable) in the 1935 movie *Mutiny on the Bounty*. Brando, who played the Christian role in the second version (1962), with Tarita playing the Tahitian lover, has fathered a son by the female leads of both versions.

Two years before Marlon Brando declined his Oscar for Best Actor for the 1972 movie *The Godfather* he had applied to the Academy of Motion Picture Arts and Sciences to replace the one he had won for *On the Waterfront* (1954), which had been stolen.

Marlon Brando–Wally Cox

Marlon Brando and Wally Cox attended the same Evanston, Illinois, elementary school (Lincoln School), and were also roommates in New York City when each was a struggling actor.

Keefe Brasselle

Actor Keefe Brasselle has authored two best-selling novels: *The Barracudas* and *The CanniBalS*.

The Brave One

A writer named Robert Rich was voted an Oscar for Best Writing for the 1956 film *The Brave One*. The Oscar was accepted by Jesse Lasky, Jr. Almost twenty years later it was revealed that Robert Rich was actually Dalton Trumbo, one of the blacklisted Hollywood Ten. Trumbo finally received his Oscar from Academy President Walter Mirisch in 1974.

Rossano Brazzi

Rossano Brazzi and his father worked with the Italian underground during World War II.

Walter Brennan

Walter Brennan is the only actor to have won three Academy Awards for Best Supporting Actor. They were for *Come and Get It* (1936), *Kentucky* (1938), and *The Westerner* (1940).

In 1960 Walter Brennan had a hit record with "Dutchman's Gold," followed two years later with an even bigger hit titled "Old Rivers."

George Brent

Before he entered movies George Brent was a dispatch runner for the Irish Republican Army.

George Brent appeared in two films titled *Luxury Liner*, the first in 1918 and the second in 1933. The movies had nothing in common but their titles.

Fanny Brice

Fanny Brice made her singing debut at Keeney's Theatre in New York and won the $5.00 first prize for "When You Know You're Not Forgotten by the Girl You Can't Forget."

The Bridge at Remagen

Congressman Ken Hechler wrote the book upon which the 1969 movie *The Bridge at Remagen* was based.

The Bridge on the River Kwai

When Pierre Boulle's novel *The Bridge Over the River Kwai* was made into a movie in 1957 the word "over" in the title was changed to "on." Chances are, although the movie is one of the most popular ever made, that hardly anyone has ever noticed. Even in the credits it is erroneously stated that the movie is from the book of the same name.

The first actor announced to play Colonel Nicholson in *The Bridge on the River Kwai* was Charles Laughton. The part went to Alec Guinness, who won the Best Actor Award for his performance. Guinness had turned down the film on three occasions.

Cary Grant was offered the role of Shears in *The Bridge on the River Kwai*, but he turned the part down because he was tired of so much traveling and location shooting. It went to William Holden. The character Shears does not appear in the novel.

Jeff Bridges

Lloyd Bridges's son Jeff wrote a musical composition that was used in the soundtrack of the 1969 Dustin Hoffman–Mia Farrow movie *John and Mary*.

Bringing Up Baby–Stagecoach

In the April 10, 1937, issue of *Collier's* magazine two short stories appeared that were later adapted to the screen. "Bringing Up Baby," by Hagar Wilde, became a movie with the same title in 1938 with Cary Grant and Katharine Hepburn. "Stage to Lordsburg," by Ernest Haycox, became *Stagecoach* in 1939 with John Wayne and Claire Trevor.

Barbara Britton

Barbara Britton appeared on the TV quiz show *The $64,000 Question* as "The Revlon Girl," replacing the original one, Wendy Barrie.

Herman Brix

Herman Brix, later famous as Bruce Bennett, was to play Tarzan in 1932 but he broke his shoulder. He was replaced by Johnny Weissmuller and had to wait several years to play the role.

Helen Broderick

Helen Broderick, the mother of Broderick Crawford, had fourth billing in the 1935 movie *Top Hat* and in the 1936 movie *Swing Time*.

Charles Bronson–George Burns– Richard Burton–Flip Wilson

Charles Bronson was the eleventh of fifteen children. George Burns was the ninth of twelve children. Richard Burton was the twelfth of thirteen children. Clerow "Flip" Wilson had seventeen brothers and sisters.

Charles Bronson–Jack Klugman

Up-and-coming actors Charles Bronson and Jack Klugman roomed together in a New York City boardinghouse in the late 1940s.

Geraldine Brooks

Brooke Costume Company, the largest theatrical costume firm in New York, is owned by James Stroock, father of actress Geraldine Brooks.

Louise Brooks

Although Louise Brooks received credit for playing a character named Bess, she did not appear in *The Public Enemy* (1931).

Rand Brooks

Actor Rand Brooks's wife, Lois, is the daughter of the late comedian Stan Laurel.

Jim Brown

During the climax of the 1967 movie *The Dirty Dozen,* actor Jim Brown was actually running for his life as he performed the feat of blowing up the set. No stunt double could be found who could run as fast as Brown.

Joe E. Brown

Joe E. Brown played professional baseball with St. Paul, a class AA club. One summer the New York Yankees showed interest in the future actor. His son, Joe L. Brown, became the general manager of the Pittsburgh Pirates.

Johnny Mack Brown

Johnny Mack Brown, who starred in the 1930 movie *Billy the Kid* and numerous other films, was named outstanding player of the 1926 Rose Bowl Game (he scored two touchdowns), which Alabama won 20–19. He was later elected to the National Football Foundation Hall of Fame.

Johnny Mack Brown–Myrna Loy

Johnny Mack Brown and Myrna Loy were schoolmates as young children.

Vanessa Brown

In her youth Vanessa Brown appeared on the radio series *The Quiz Kids*. Later she was a correspondent for radio's *Voice of America*.

Vanessa Brown has written several newspaper articles and a book titled *The Manpower Policies of Secretary of Labor Wilson Wirtz*.

Roscoe Lee Browne

Roscoe Lee Browne, who has appeared on Broadway and in such movies as *The World's*

Greatest Athlete (1975) and *Logan's Run* (1976), set a world's record in 1951 at Paris for the 800-meter run. He has also twice won the 1000-yard championship.

Before turning to acting Roscoe Lee Browne taught literature and French at Lincoln University.

Edgar Buchanan

Edgar Buchanan played a dentist in the 1941 movie *Texas*, a part he had rehearsed for ten years, having been an established dentist himself.

Bugs Bunny

Bugs Bunny was originally called Happy Rabbit prior to his debut in the 1940 cartoon *A Wild Hare*.

In a scene from the 1934 movie *It Happened One Night* Clark Gable eats a carrot. This single scene gave Bob Clampett his inspiration for the cartoon character Bugs Bunny.

Billie Burke

Billie Burke was the daughter of a circus clown who worked for the Barnum & Bailey Circus.

In *The Wizard of Oz* Billie Burke's singing voice in the Munchkinland number was actually dubbed by Lorraine Bridges.

George Burns and Gracie Allen

At the beginning of the careers of comedians George Burns and Gracie Allen it was

Gracie who played the "straight" member of the act. Later, after reversing the roles, the couple won fame.

Raymond Burr

Raymond Burr played a reporter in the 1956 movie *Godzilla* and also narrated the film.

In 1965 Raymond Burr bought his own South Pacific island. It is 165 miles northeast of Suva in Fiji, and it is named Naitamba. He now lives on the 3000-acre island.

Ellen Burstyn

Ellen Burstyn, who won the Best Actress Award for *Alice Doesn't Live Here Anymore* (1974), appeared on the Jackie Gleason TV show in the 1950s holding up billboards to advertise Old Gold cigarettes. In the 1960s she played Dr. Kate Bartok on the TV soap *The Doctors* under the name Ellen McRae.

Richard Burton

Richard Burton was born in the south Wales village of Pontypridd in 1925. In 1940 Thomas Woodward was born there. Woodward is today better known as singer Tom Jones.

At age fifteen Richard Burton won a prize fight. He later won a scholarship to Exeter College, Oxford University. He turned down a position as don at Oxford University.

Welsh rugby star Bleddyn Williams stated in his autobiography *Rugger, My Life* that

Richard Burton could have been one of the best wing forwards ever to come out of Wales.

The New York City Botanical Garden has named a rose for Richard Burton.

Francis X. Bushman

Francis X. Bushman, a popular actor among the female moviegoers, died on August 24, 1966, which was exactly forty years to the day after another screen idol, Rudolph Valentino, had passed away.

Butch Cassidy and the Sundance Kid

Steve McQueen, Marlon Brando, and Warren Beatty were all considered for the part of the Sundance Kid in the 1969 movie *Butch Cassidy and the Sundance Kid,* but the job went to Robert Redford, the man that director George Roy Hill wanted.

Rhett Butler

Gary Cooper, Errol Flynn, Warner Baxter, Basil Rathbone, and Ronald Colman were all considered for the part of Rhett Butler in *Gone With The Wind*. The American public virtually demanded Clark Gable. 1939 brought the decision.

Red Buttons

Aaron Chwatt was given his stage name of Red Buttons when as a lad he first worked at Dinty Moore's tavern in the Bronx as a singer/

waiter. He had to wear a uniform with forty-eight buttons and with his red hair, people began calling him Red Buttons.

Edd Byrnes–Henry Winkler

Edd "Kookie" Byrnes, the hottest "teenager" on TV in the 1950s, and Henry "Fonzie" Winkler, the hottest "teenager" of the 1970s, both played in stage productions of *Hamlet* prior to appearing on television.

C

James Caan

During his high school days James Caan was captain of both the basketball and the baseball teams. He also served as president of his class. Prior to becoming an actor he was a rodeo rider.

James Caan–Robert De Niro

James Caan and Robert De Niro, both of whom appeared in the 1974 movie *The Godfather, Part II,* attended the same Manhattan high school, Rhodes High.

Sebastian Cabot

Prior to becoming an actor, Sebastian Cabot served as a chauffer to British actor Frank Pettingell.

Sid Caesar

Comedian Sid Caesar played saxophone for the Charlie Spivak band for a short time in the 1940s.

James Cagney

James Cagney's German instructor at Stuyvesant High School in New York was the father of future director and screenwriter Joseph L. Mankiewicz.

Two of James Cagney's brothers, Harry and Edward, became doctors.

James Cagney's first theatrical performance was as a female impersonator, a chorus girl in *Every Sailor* (1920).

James Cagney accepted no salary for his portrayal of George M. Cohan in *The Seven Little Foys* (1955). In his struggling days, Cagney was befriended by Foy many times, and this was Cagney's way of symbolically repaying him.

James Cagney's home in Martha's Vineyard, Massachusetts, contains a staircase that appeared in his 1942 movie *Yankee Doodle Dandy*.

James Cagney–Joan Blondell

James Cagney and Joan Blondell made their screen debuts in the same picture, *Sin-*

ner's Holiday (1930), after they were discovered on Broadway by Al Jolson, who brought them to the attention of Warner Bros.

James Cagney–Rita Hayworth

In the 1920s James Cagney attended the Professional Dancing School in Hollywood. The daughter of the owner was Margarita Cansino, later to be known as Rita Hayworth.

Michael Caine

British actor Michael Caine has never taken the time nor does he have the inclination to learn to drive an automobile.

Michael Caine's real name is Maurice Micklewhite. He took the name Caine from a theater marquee advertising the 1954 film *The Caine Mutiny*. British TV actor Stanley Hunter is the brother of Michael Caine.

Rory Calhoun

Actor Rory Calhoun was arrested and sentenced to three years at the Federal Reformatory at El Reno, Oklahoma, at the age of eighteen.

California Split

Director Robert Altman's 1974 movie *California Split* was the first movie to utilize eight-track stereo.

Rod Cameron

In his youth Rod Cameron helped to build the Holland Tunnel in New York.

For a time Rod Cameron was a stand-in for Fred MacMurray. He also served as a stunt double for Buck Jones in Western movies.

Rod Cameron married Angela Alves-Lico and later Angela's mother, making them his third and fourth wives.

In 1972, at the age of fifty-nine, veteran screen actor Rod Cameron fell overboard from a chartered boat off the Miami coast while inebriated. He treaded water for three hours until he was rescued. Since that day he has not had a drop of alcohol.

Cancel My Reservation

When Radio City Music Hall had to close for a couple of days in 1972 due to a labor dispute, the film showing there was *Cancel My Reservation*.

Dyan Cannon

Actress Dyan Cannon, previously the wife of Cary Grant and mother of his only child (Jennifer), once held the title of Miss West Seattle.

Eddie Cantor

It was supposedly comedian Eddie Cantor who coined the title "March of Dimes," the campaign for the National Foundation of Infantile **Paralysis**, which was founded by President Franklin D. Roosevelt.

Eddie Cantor always ate cornflakes with milk for dinner, even when he went out to high-class restaurants.

Eddie Cantor–Jimmy Durante

Like two trains passing in the night, two unknowns crossed paths early in their careers. At the Coney Island Saloon Eddie Cantor had a job as a singer/waiter; the piano player there was a young man named Jimmy Durante.

Yakima Canutt

Famed stuntman and second unit director Yakima Canutt was the World Champion Rodeo Rider from 1917 to 1923.

Al Capone

Desi Arnaz and Sonny Capone were high school classmates. Desilu Productions later was to produce *The Untouchables* series, which prominently displayed Sonny's father, Al Capone, as the boss of the racketeers.

Frank Capra

Movie director Frank Capra was part of a team granted a patent in 1939 for a remote-control guidance system by which planes were directed to release bombs by radio.

Captain Blood

In 1935 Errol Flynn played the title role in the movie *Captain Blood*. Twenty-seven years later his son Sean played the lead in *Son of Captain Blood*. Sean later became a photo-journalist and now is missing, presumed dead, in Southeast Asia.

Harry Carey

Harry Carey was the son of a New York City judge. Prior to making his screen debut at age forty, he studied law and wrote several plays.

Harry Carey–John Kerr

Before becoming an actor Harry Carey practiced law; before becoming a lawyer John Kerr was an actor.

Hoagy Carmichael

Prior to becoming a successful composer, Hoagy Carmichael was a lawyer.

Art Carney

Art Carney was once a singer with Horace Heidt's orchestra.

The night before Art Carney was drafted into the U.S. Army (March 15, 1944), he portrayed General Eisenhower on the radio series *Report to the Nation*.

Art Carney's right leg is almost one inch shorter than his left leg. This was caused by a piece of shrapnel that put him in the hospital for nine months when he was fighting in France during World War II.

Gino Carrado

Gino Carrado played a waiter in the films *Top Hat* (1935), *Gone with the Wind* (1939), *Casablanca* (1943), and *My Wild Irish Rose* (1947), among others.

Leo Carrillo

Carlos Antonio Carillo, the great-grandfather of actor Leo Carrillo, served as governor of California in 1837.

Diahann Carroll

Diahann Carroll won a Metropolitan Opera scholarship when she was but ten years old. Yet in the 1959 movie *Porgy and Bess* Loulie Jean Norman dubbed her singing.

John Carroll

During World War II John Carroll was an Army Air Corps pilot in North Africa and in a crash broke his back, but lived.

Actors John Carroll and Errol Flynn once traveled to Cuba to visit with revolutionary leader Fidel Castro in Cuba's Sierra Maestra mountains.

Jack Carson

While playing football for Carleton College, 6′ 2″ Jack Carson once tackled football great Bronko Nagurski.

Johnny Carson

When Johnny Carson visited California after his high school graduation he was selected from an audience to assist Orson Welles in a magic act. Carson performed magic for several years in his youth as "The Great Carsoni."

Sunset Carson

Western star Sunset Carson won the title of All-Around Champion Cowboy of South America two years in a row, 1941 and 1942.

Enrico Caruso

Several greats were in San Francisco the day of the famous 1906 earthquake. John Barrymore said he slept through it, and Enrico Caruso was so frightened that he swore he would never return to the City by the Bay. He kept his promise. Future actor Warner Baxter and his parents' family lost all of their possessions in the fire that followed.

Enrico Caruso was paid $250,000 to appear in a 1917 film. The movie lost a bundle because it was a silent movie and no one could hear the great singer's voice.

Casablanca

Everyone knows that Humphrey Bogart, Ingrid Bergman, and Paul Henreid played the lead roles in *Casablanca*. Originally set for those roles were Ronald Reagan, Ann Sheridan, and Dennis Morgan.

Casablanca debuted at New York's Hollywood Theater on Thanksgiving Day, 1942, just eighteen days after the invasion of Casablanca by Allied forces. For Academy Award purposes it was considered a 1943 release.

S. Z. Sakall was mistakenly billed as S. K. Sakall in *Casablanca*.

Adriana Caselotti

The high notes of Jack Haley's singing of "If I Only Had a Heart" in *The Wizard of Oz* were actually sung by Adriana Caselotti.

Fidel Castro

In his youth Fidel Castro appeared in a few Xavier Cugat movies such as *Holiday in Mexico* (1946).

Cat Ballou

Kirk Douglas turned down a dual role in the 1965 movie *Cat Ballou*. Lee Marvin won the Academy Award for playing Kid Sheleen and Tim Strawn.

Joan Caulfield

Joan Caulfield was a model who appeared on the cover of *Life* magazine (May 11, 1942) before turning to an acting career.

Dick Cavett

Dick Cavett was once a copyboy for *Time* magazine. He has written comedy material for Jack Paar, Johnny Carson, and Jerry Lewis.

Centaur Pictures

In 1911 William and David Horsley decided to begin shooting their pictures in a location other than New Jersey. It would be in either Florida or California. A flip of a coin was made. California won, so William and David moved out there and founded the first movie studio in Hollywood, Centaur Pictures.

George Chakiris

In the 1961 movie *West Side Story* George Chakiris played Bernardo, the leader of the Puerto Rican gang, the Sharks. Russ Tamblyn played Riff, the leader of the Jets. On the London stage Chakiris played the leader of the Jets.

Marilyn Chambers

Porno queen Marilyn Chambers of *Behind the Green Door* fame, was once a model on boxes of Ivory Soap detergent, seen holding a baby.

Marge Champion

The model for Walt Disney's Snow White was Marjorie Belcher, later known as Marge Champion.

Jeff Chandler

Jeff Chandler was the voice of Mr. Boynton on the radio program *Our Miss Brooks*.

Jeff Chandler—Alan Hale

Jeff Chandler played Cochise in *Broken Arrow* (1950), *The Battle of Apache Pass* (1952), and *Taza, Son of Cochise* (1954). Alan Hale played Little John in *Robin Hood* (1922), *The Adventures of Robin Hood* (1938), and *The Rogues of Sherwood Forest* (1950).

Lon Chaney

Silent star Lon Chaney was the son of deaf-mute parents.

Lon Chaney once wrote an article for the *Encyclopaedia Britannica* on the subject of theatrical makeup.

Lon Chaney, Jr.

In various films Lon Chaney, Jr., played the Frankenstein Monster, the Wolf Man, Dracula, and the Mummy. He was the first to be offered the lead role in the remakes of *The Hunchback of Notre Dame* and *The Phantom of the Opera* but he declined.

Lon Chaney, Jr., died on Friday the 13th (July 13, 1973).

Carol Channing

As a teenager, Carol Channing danced with the San Francisco Ballet.

Carol Channing's father, George, was editor-in-chief of Christian Science publications and was head lecturer for the organization.

Charlie Chaplin

Woody Allen, who has been compared to Charlie Chaplin many times, is not the first comic actor to have a comic strip about him. In 1916 Ed Carey wrote the comic strip *Pa's Imported Son-in-Law* about the adventures of Charlie Chaplin.

Charlie Chaplin was the first actor to appear on the cover of *Time* magazine (July 6, 1925).

Charlie Chaplin's last wife was playwright Eugene O'Neill's daughter Oona.

Charlie Chaplin was knighted at Buckingham Palace, only three miles from the slums where he grew up.

Charlie Chaplin was officially banned from the United States in the early 1950s for his political beliefs. In 1972 he returned to be awarded a Special Oscar.

Charlie Chaplin, along with Geoffrey Parsons and John Turner, composed the 1954 ballad hit song "Smile."

Charlie Chaplin wrote and directed the

1967 movie *A Countess from Hong Kong* with Marlon Brando and Sophia Loren. In the movie, he made his final film appearance in a cameo role as a seasick steward.

Charles Chaplin Studio

Herb Alpert's A&M Record Company complex is built on the grounds of the former Charles Chaplin Studio in Los Angeles.

Geraldine Chaplin

Playwright Eugene O'Neill is the grandfather of actress Geraldine Chaplin, who is the daughter of Charlie Chaplin.

Oona Chaplin

It has been guessed that at the time of Charlie Chaplin's death, his wife Oona became the richest widow in the world. Because of Chaplin's shrewd gold investments her worth is estimated at $100 million.

Marguerite Chapman

After her 1960 retirement from motion pictures Marguerite Chapman became an accomplished painter who has many of her canvases on display in California art galleries.

The Charge of the Light Brigade

Anita Louise was to play opposite Errol Flynn in the 1936 movie *The Charge of the*

Light Brigade but the part went to Olivia de Havilland.

Cyd Charisse

Cyd Charisse broke her leg and lost her part in the 1948 movie *Easter Parade* to Ann Miller. Miss Charisse lost another part to Leslie Caron in the 1951 film *An American in Paris* when she became pregnant.

Charlie Chan

Charlie Chan, a Hawaiian policeman of Chinese ancestry, was played on radio by Walter Connolly, Ed Begley, Cy Kendall, and Santos Ortega. In the movies he was played by George Kuwa, Kamiyama Sojin, E. L. Park, Warner Oland, Sidney Toler, and Roland Winters. On TV he was played by J. Carroll Naish and Ross Martin. On Broadway Harold Huber played Chan. Yet not one of these actors is Chinese; and George Kuwa and Kamiyama Sojin were actually Japanese.

Leo Carrillo and Noah Beery both tested for the part of Charlie Chan after Warner Oland died in 1938. Sidney Toler was then given the role of the famous Oriental detective.

Cheerleaders

Dyan Cannon, Lily Tomlin, Raquel Welch, Eydie Gormé, Dinah Shore, Cheryl Ladd, Ann-Margret, and William Powell were all cheerleaders in high school. Jimmy Stewart was a cheerleader at Princeton University.

Maurice Chevalier

In his youth Maurice Chevalier was a sparring partner for Georges Carpentier.

Maurice Chevalier was wounded in 1914 and spent over two years as a German prisoner of war at Alten Grabow prison camp.

In 1951 the U.S. State Department declared Maurice Chevalier potentially dangerous to the security of the United States because he had signed a petition against nuclear weapons called the Stockholm Appeal.

Chief John Big Tree

Chief John Big Tree (real name: Isaac Johnny John) appeared in several Westerns such as *Stagecoach* (1939) and *She Wore a Yellow Ribbon* (1949). He was also the model for the "Indian Head" nickel which first appeared in 1912.

Julie Christie–Frank Sinatra

Julie Christie received only $7500 for her Oscar-winning performance in *Darling* (1965). Frank Sinatra received only $8000 for his Oscar-winning performance in *From Here to Eternity* (1953).

William Christopher

William Christopher, who plays Father Mulcahy on the TV series *M*A*S*H*, claims to be a descendant of Paul Revere.

Winston Churchill

Ethel Barrymore once turned down a marriage proposal from Winston Churchill.

Eduardo Ciannelli

Movie tough guy Eduardo Ciannelli had been a doctor and an opera singer prior to appearing on Broadway and later in films.

Cimarron

The only Western to win an Oscar for Best Picture was *Cimarron* (1930/1931).

Circus performers

The mother of Bud Abbott was once a bareback rider with the Ringling Brothers Circus. Donald O'Connor's parents were both circus performers, his mother Effie, like Bud Abbott's, was a bareback rider. Child actress Margaret O'Brien's father also rode in a circus.

Citizen Kane

Orson Welles, Ray Collins, Ruth Warrick, Joseph Cotten, Agnes Moorehead, and Paul Stewart all made their screen debuts in *Citizen Kane* (1941).

City Lights

Jean Harlow played an unbilled extra in the 1931 Charlie Chaplin classic *City Lights*.

Dane Clark

Actor Dane Clark earned a law degree from St. Johns.

Dick Clark

Dick Clark and his wife Carey were married on July 7, 1977, in a ceremony that started at 7:00 P.M. and ended at 7:17 P.M. They were married by the father of singer John Davidson. In Burbank in September 1978 the U.S. Post Office assigned Clark Box 7777. He had not requested it.

Petula Clark

Petula Clark turned down the role of Neely O'Hara in the 1967 movie *Valley of the Dolls*. The part went to Patty Duke.

Cleopatra

Elizabeth Taylor was the first person to demand and receive $1,000,000 for making a motion picture, *Cleopatra* (1963).

Laurence Olivier turned down the part of Julius Caesar in *Cleopatra*. Peter Finch assumed the role and completed some work before Trevor Howard was considered. Rex Harrison eventually played Caesar.

Montgomery Clift

Montgomery Clift was the great grandson of Major Robert Anderson, commander of Fort Sumter at the outbreak of the Civil War.

In his youth Montgomery Clift was a John Robert Powers model and did some ads for Arrow shirts.

Montgomery Clift turned down roles in *Sunset Boulevard, Shane, On the Waterfront, East of Eden, Moby Dick, Friendly Persuasion,* and *Cat on a Hot Tin Roof* among others.

Lee J. Cobb

Lee J. Cobb was a member of the Civil Air Patrol as a pilot during World War II.

Iron Eyes Cody

Iron Eyes Cody, in films since the 1920s, has authored several books about Indians. He appeared in the 1975 movie *Hearts of the West* as a cowboy.

Barry Coe

Actor Barry Coe married Jorvnn Kristiansen, Miss Norway of 1959.

Frank Coghlan, Jr.

Frank Coghlan, Jr., played Captain Marvel's alter ego, Billy Batson, in the 1941 serial *The Adventures of Captain Marvel.* Today he is a retired U.S. Navy Lt. Commander.

George M. Cohan

George M. Cohan may have been a great composer and producer but could he recognize talent? James Cagney once gave an audition for Cohan as a youth but the Broadway impresario rejected him. Later Cohan fired Clark Gable from his 1929 play *Gambling*.

James Cagney portrayed George M. Cohan in two different movies: *Yankee Doodle Dandy* (1942) and *The Seven Little Foys* (1955).

George M. Cohan–Bob Hope

George M. Cohan and Bob Hope are the only entertainers ever to have been awarded the Congressional Medal of Honor for their nonmilitary work.

Claudette Colbert

If one watches closely in the films of Claudette Colbert it is obvious that she preferred her left side for all profile shots. Camera shots from her right side are very rare.

Anita Colby

Anita "The Face" Colby, for a time the world's highest-paid model ($50.00 per hour in the mid-1930s), was the technical advisor for the 1944 movie *Cover Girl*.

Charles Collingwood

Newsman Charles Collingwood, awarded an MBE from Great Britain, is the husband of actress Louise Allbritton.

Patrick Collins

TV actor Patrick Collins, who appeared on *Supertrain,* spent six years of silence in a monastery as a monk.

Bud Collyer

Clayton "Bud" Collyer, the host of TV's *Beat the Clock,* was the radio voice of Superman.

Jerry Colonna

Jerry Colonna was at one time a trombone player in John Scott Trotter's band.

Colors

Singer Johnny Cash wears black when he performs; Jayne Mansfield usually wore pink. Mae West wears white whenever she is to be seen by the public.

Columbo

Veteran character actor Thomas Mitchell played Lieutenant Columbo on the Broadway stage in 1962. The creators of the TV series, Richard Levinson and William Link, wanted Bing Crosby to play Columbo for their pilot movie but he was unavailable. The part then went to Peter Falk.

Come Back, Little Sheba

Shirley Booth won an Academy Award for her movie debut role of Lola in the 1952 movie

Come Back Little Sheba. The part was initially turned down by Bette Davis.

Comic strip characters

Groucho Marx (born Julius) was named Groucho after a comic strip character named Groucho Monk. Mickey Rooney as a youth used the name Mickey McGuire taken from a comic strip character in Fontaine Fox's *The Toonerville Trolley.* Rooney's real name is Joe Yule, Jr. Bing Crosby, whose real first name was Harry, was nicknamed Bing after a character named Bingo in a strip titled *Bingville Bugle.*

Merrill Connally

Bit actor Merrill Connally, who has appeared in *The Sugarland Express* (1974) and *Close Encounters of the Third Kind* (1977), is the brother of former Texas Governor John Connally.

Sean Connery

Sean Connery receives a 20 percent disability pension (nine shillings a week) from the Royal Navy due to ulcers he acquired in the British Navy. He once worked as a coffin polisher.

Sean Connery was Scotland's representative to the Mr. Universe Pageant held in London in 1953. He finished in the top ten.

In 1967 Sean Connery's kid brother, Neil,

appeared in a low-budget movie. Its title was *Operation Kid Brother.*

Sean Connery claimed he would never play James Bond again, but was lured back for his final appearance in the 1971 motion picture *Diamonds Are Forever* by a $1,000,000 acting fee, which he donated to the Scottish International Education Trust.

The Conqueror

Howard Hughes's 1956 bomb *The Conqueror*, which starred John Wayne and Susan Hayward, only returned $4.5 million of its $6 million cost in its initial release. As if this wasn't bad enough, recluse Hughes spent nearly $12 million over several years trying to buy up every known print of the film. Hughes liked to watch his unplanned disaster movie.

Robert Conrad

Athletic-minded Robert Conrad fought thirty-two amateur boxing matches in his early days in Chicago.

In August 1978 Robert Conrad became the first civilian pilot to solo in the U.S. Navy A4 jet fighter.

William Conrad

William Conrad was promoted several times in school and graduated from junior college at the age of sixteen.

William Conrad, who played heavy-set de-

tective Frank Cannon on television, also narrated TV's *The Fugitive.*

While fishing in a tournament off the coast
of Hawaii in 1977 William Conrad landed the
largest marlin, a 683-pounder.

Tim Conway

Comedian Tim Conway changed his name
from Tom Conway in order not to be confused
with an actor of the same name, who was
George Sanders's brother. Sanders was the family name.

Tom Conway–George Sanders

Brothers Tom Conway and George Sanders were the sons of the British Consul of Russia in the early 1900s.

Jackie Coogan

As a popular child-star Jackie Coogan had
a candy named after him, "Jackie Coogan Salt-
ed Peanuts," manufactured by a Cleveland
firm.

In 1924 Jackie Coogan was being paid
$22,500 per week. His parents gave him a
weekly allowance of $6.25. A landmark court
case resulted in protection of the incomes of
child actors. The law was passed on May 4,
1939, and became known thereafter as the Coogan Act. When Coogan turned twenty-one
there was less than $150,000 left from the mil-
lions he had earned.

During World War II Jackie Coogan served as a glider pilot.

Tommy Cook

Former child actor Tommy Cook is today one of the better-known tennis pros in California.

Cool Hand Luke–The French Connection

In the 1967 movie *Cool Hand Luke*, based on the book by Donn Pearce, the author played a prisoner named Sailor. In the 1971 movie *The French Connection* the man who helped inspire the movie, Eddie Egan, appeared in the film. He later became a regular on the TV series *Joe Forrester*.

Gary Cooper

Gary Cooper, born Frank James Cooper in 1901, was the son of Charles Cooper, a Montana State Supreme Court judge.

Gary Cooper spent several summers as a guide in Yellowstone National Park.

In 1928 Gary Cooper appeared in a sequel to the 1926 silent version of *Beau Geste* which was titled *Beau Sabreur*. Cooper would later star in the title role of the 1939 version, making him the only actor to appear in a sequel and then a remake.

Gary Cooper taught his wife Veronica (known as "Rocky") how to shoot a gun in 1939. Several years later she won the California Women's Skeet-Shooting Championship.

Gary Cooper portrayed Lou Gehrig in the 1942 movie *Pride of the Yankees* although he had never played in a baseball game before in his life.

Gladys Cooper

Gladys Cooper was the British soldiers' favorite pin-up girl of World War I.

Jackie Cooper

Former child actor Jackie Cooper has won Emmy Awards for directing episodes of the TV series *M*A*S*H* and *The White Shadow*.

Merian C. Cooper

Producer Merian C. Cooper attended Annapolis for three years, spent time in the National Guard, and after U.S. entry into World War I enlisted in the Army's air service. In the last months of the war he was shot down and taken prisoner. He joined the Polish Army in 1919 and was shot down by Russians in 1920. He escaped in 1921. Twelve years later he produced *King Kong*.

Coppola family

One family walked away with four Academy Awards in one evening. Francis Ford Coppola received three Oscars for *The Godfather, Part II*. His father, Carmine, shared Best Original Score with Nino Rota. The family missed a fifth Oscar when Coppola's sister, Talia Shire, lost in the Best Supporting Actress category to Ingrid Bergman for *Murder on the Orient Express* (1974).

James J. Corbett

Ever wonder who the first movie star was? The first person put under contract to appear in a movie was heavyweight champion James J. Corbett, by Thomas Edison in August 1894.

Ellen Corby

Ellen Corby (Grandma Walton on the TV series *The Waltons*) began working in Hollywood as a script girl. She co-wrote two screenplays for Hopalong Cassidy films. She later played a script girl in the 1968 film *The Legend of Lylah Clare*.

Wendell Corey

In 1966 actor Wendell Corey ran unsuccessfully for Congressman from California.

Bill Cosby

As a student at Temple University Bill Cosby was scouted by Emlen Tunnell while playing halfback. Tunnell predicted that Cosby could have played professional football had he chosen to.

Bill Cosby received his Doctorate in Education in 1977.

Lou Costello

Five-foot-four Lou Costello was a semi-pro basketball player prior to becoming a professional comedian. He was a state champion foul shooter for a team in New Jersey. In twelve amateur boxing matches he won eleven and had one draw.

One of Lou Costello's first jobs in Hollywood was as an MGM stunt-double for actress Dolores Del Rio.

The Country Doctor

Will Rogers had signed to do the part of Dr. Allan Dafoe in a film about the Dionne quintuplets titled *The Country Doctor*, but he was killed in an airplane crash with Wiley Post in 1935. The film was completed by Jean Hersholt in 1936 and led to the Dr. Christian movie series.

The Country Girl

Jennifer Jones became pregnant; Greta Garbo turned it down; and *The Country Girl* went to Grace Kelly who won the 1954 Best Actress Award for her performance.

The Courage of Lassie

In the 1946 movie *The Courage of Lassie*, starring Elizabeth Taylor, Lassie was neither seen nor mentioned. Taylor's dog in the film was named Bill.

Noel Coward

Noel Coward wrote the theme song used by one of radio's most popular shows, *Mr. Keen, Tracer of Lost Persons.* The song was "Someday I'll Find You."

Wally Cox

Eleanor Frances Atkinson, the mother of Wally Cox, wrote mystery stories under the pen name Eleanor Blake.

Buster Crabbe

While in high school, future Olympian and Tarzan Larry "Buster" Crabbe won sixteen letters in various sports.

James Craig

James Craig was an All-Southern end for Rice University where he was a medical student.

James Craig, born James Henry Meador, adopted his screen name from a role he played in the 1936 movie *Craig's Wife.*

Jeanne Crain

Jeanne Crain was Miss Long Beach in 1941 and was a runner-up in the Miss America contest.

Bob Crane

Hogan's Heroes star Bob Crane was a drummer with the Connecticut Symphony Orchestra.

Joan Crawford

A contest at MGM was held to rename Lucille Le Sueur in 1925. The winner chose the name Joan Arden, until it was discovered that there was already an actress at MGM named Joan Arden, and so Lucille's name was changed to Joan Crawford.

Joan Crawford became the daughter-in-law of Mary Pickford when she married Douglas Fairbanks, Jr.

Joan Crawford doubled for Norma Shearer in the 1925 movie *Lady of the Night*.

Joan Crawford, who became a member of Pepsi Cola's board of directors after marrying Alfred Steele, had previously posed for Coca-Cola advertisements in the 1930s.

When cartoonist Milton Caniff created the character Dragon Lady, foe of Terry Lee, for his comic strip *Terry and the Pirates*, he modeled the Oriental villainess after the face of actress Joan Crawford.

Joan Crawford was the first choice for the Deborah Kerr role in *From Here to Eternity* (1953) but she would not accept second billing to Burt Lancaster.

Joan Crawford appeared in four episodes of the TV soap opera *The Secret Storm* in 1968, replacing her adopted daughter, Christina.

Joseph Crehan

Joseph Crehan portrayed Ulysses S. Grant in four movies: *Union Pacific* (1939), *The Adventures of Mark Twain* (1941), *They Died with Their Boots On* (1942), and *Silver River* (1948).

Joseph Crehan's photograph is seen on a political poster under which the two gangs run in the 1961 movie *West Side Story*.

Kathy Cronkite

Kathy Cronkite, who has appeared in *The Trial of Billy Jack* (1974) and *Network* (1976), is the daughter of Walter Cronkite.

Hume Cronyn

Actor Hume Cronyn was selected for the Canadian Olympic boxing team in 1932.

Bing Crosby

Bing Crosby's great-grandfather Nathaniel Crosby was one of the founders of Portland, Oregon, and Olympia, Washington.

At Webster Grade School in Spokane Bing Crosby played on the football, basketball, and baseball teams. By the age of twelve he had won seven medals for swimming. In high school he played baseball and football, and in his very first swim meet he won nine first places and two second places. He was also color blind.

During World War II, while on a USO tour, Bing Crosby and his jeep driver found themselves in the wrong German town, behind enemy lines.

The Oscar that Bing Crosby won for *Going My Way* (1944) is kept at Gonzaga University, the school he attended in Spokane.

The S.S. *Nathaniel Crosby* was a liberty

ship launched in 1944, christened for Bing Crosby's grandfather, a pioneer of the ocean route from China to the West Coast.

The granddaughter of Bing Crosby, Denise Crosby, posed semi-nude for *Playboy* magazine.

Bing Crosby–Clark Gable

Because their ears were so large, both Bing Crosby and Clark Gable often had them taped back while making movies.

Bing Crosby–Pat O'Brien

Bing Crosby and Pat O'Brien founded the Del Mar racetrack near San Diego in 1937.

Gary Crosby

Bing Crosby's son Gary, born in 1933, was named for actor Gary Cooper who was a good friend of Bing's. Gary Cooper in turn took his first name from Gary, Indiana, where Karl Malden (whose real name is Malden Sekulovich) was born.

Kathryn Grant Crosby

Kathryn Grant Crosby once finished second in a Miss Texas pageant.

The Crowded Sky

In the 1960 movie *The Crowded Sky* Dana Andrews played the pilot of a passenger aircraft that collides in mid-air with a Navy fighter flown by Efrem Zimbalist, Jr. The fighter pilot is killed in the collision. In the movie *Airport 1975* Andrews plays the pilot of a Beech Baron that collides in mid-air with a Boeing 747 flown by Efrem Zimbalist, Jr. Andrews is killed in that collision. Thus, after fifteen years, their roles were reversed.

Robert Cummings

Orville Wright was the godfather of Robert Orville Cummings.

Robert Cummings, born in 1908, has authored a book titled *How To Stay Young and Vital*.

Whenever Robert Cummings is to play a dramatic role he is billed as Robert Cummings. When he is to play a comedy, however, he is billed as Bob Cummings.

Ken Curtis

Ken Curtis, who played Festus on TV's *Gunsmoke*, once sang with The Sons of the Pioneers and with the Tommy Dorsey band.

Tony Curtis

As a young lad Tony Curtis learned to imitate Cary Grant's voice, which he did effectively in *Some Like It Hot* (1959). During World War II Curtis saw submarine duty in the Pacific. The only movie onboard was Grant's 1939 film *Gunga Din*, which the crew saw so often that the men could recite it from memory. Curtis filled in Grant's lines for practice.

Tony Curtis has appeared in movies under the names James Curtis, Anthony Curtis, and Tony Curtis.

Tony Curtis has worn a straitjacket in three films: *Houdini* (1953), *The Great Race* (1965), and *The Boston Strangler* (1968). However, he rarely wears makeup.

Tony Curtis wrote the best-selling 1977 novel *Kid Andrew Cody & Julie Sparrow*.

Tony Curtis–Peter O'Toole–Richard Denning

Tony Curtis, Peter O'Toole, and Richard Denning all saw submarine service while in the military in World War II.

Michael Curtiz

Director Michael Curtiz was a member of the Hungarian fencing team at the 1912 Stockholm Olympics.

D

Arlene Dahl

In 1963 Arlene Dahl wrote the book *Always Ask a Man*, her first of twelve beauty books.

James Daly

Dorothy Hogan Daly, the mother of actor James Daly, was once an employee of the CIA. Her other son David was an FBI agent.

The late James Daly was the father-in-law of actor Georg Stanford Brown.

Dorothy Dandridge

As a child Dorothy Dandridge appeared as an extra in the 1937 Marx Brothers movie *A Day at the Races*.

Dorothy Dandridge once was a singer with Jimmy Luceford's band.

Bebe Daniels

Silent star Bebe Daniels received a Presidential Medal of Freedom in 1946 for her efforts in entertaining servicemen overseas during World War II. She was the first female civilian to enter Normandy after the D-Day invasion.

Michael Dante

Actor Michael Dante, whose real name is Ralph Vitti, once played professional baseball under the name of Ralph Pucci.

Dark Victory

Dark Victory (1939) was originally planned for Greta Garbo. She preferred to do *Anna Karenina,* and the part went to Bette Davis.

Linda Darnell

Linda Darnell was turned down for the title role in *Song of Bernadette* (1944); however, she did play the unbilled part of the Virgin Mary.

In 1965 Linda Darnell died of burns suffered when her home caught fire. Earlier in her career she "died" by burning in two of her movies: *Hangover Square* (1945) and *Anna and the King of Siam* (1946).

Jane Darwell

Jane Darwell, born Patti Woodward, was the daughter of W. R. Woodward, the president of the Louisville Southern Railroad.

David Copperfield

Louis B. Mayer wanted Jackie Cooper for his 1935 movie *David Copperfield* but Freddie Bartholomew got the part.

Marion Davies

In high school in Brooklyn Marion Davies was captain of a championship basketball team.

The first photograph transmitted by telegraph wire (April 1925) was sent from San Francisco to New York and was about Marion Davies receiving a makeup box from Louis B. Mayer.

Bette Davis

Bette Davis was originally cast as Elizabeth in the 1931 classic *Frankenstein*, but after costume tests the part was given to Mae Clarke.

Bette Davis has been the only female president of the Academy of Motion Picture Arts and Sciences. She resigned the same year that she was elected, 1942.

On September 21, 1962, Bette Davis advertised in a trade paper for a job.

Clifton Davis

Clifton Davis, star of TV's *That's My Mama,* composed the 1971 hit song "Never Can Say Goodbye" by the Jackson Five.

Ossie Davis

Actor and playwright Ossie Davis spoke at the funerals of both Malcolm X and Martin Luther King, Jr., two men with totally different philosophies but two men whom Davis felt had helped the cause of blacks.

Dennis Day–Penny Singleton

McNulty is the real last name of both singer Dennis Day and actress Penny Singleton, although they are not related.

Doris Day

Doris Day's mother named her daughter Doris after silent screen star Doris Kenyon. Years later Doris Day became a neighbor of Doris Kenyon.

Doris von Kappelhoff was renamed Doris Day by bandleader Barney Rapp because he liked the way she sang "Day After Day."

Doris Day was a singer with both the Bob Crosby and Les Brown bands.

In a recent court case Doris Day was

awarded the largest amount ever granted in California for a civil suit: $22,835,646.

Doris Day–Lucille Ball

As young ladies, both Doris Day and Lucille Ball were victims of automobile accidents in which both experienced serious leg injuries. In each case the attending physician said that they would never walk again.

Doris Day–Marlon Brando

Doris Day and Marlon Brando share the same birthday, April 3, 1924.

Laraine Day

Laraine Day's Mormon grandfather had fifty-two children, by more than one wife.

Laraine Day was married to former Brooklyn Dodgers manager Leo Durocher.

At one time Laraine Day had her own syndicated newspaper column.

The Day the Earth Stood Still

Claude Rains was originally picked to play Klaatu in the 1951 classic *The Day the Earth Stood Still*. Michael Rennie eventually played the part.

Gort, the robot in *The Day the Earth Stood Still*, was played by J. Lockard Martin, the doorman at Grauman's Chinese Theatre. He was selected for his 7′ 7″ height, but he was so weak that he couldn't lift Patricia Neal.

James Dean

While a student at Fairmount High School in Fairmount, Indiana, James Dean won a statewide speech contest. He finished sixth in a national contest. He also lettered in baseball, ran the hurdles in track, played on the basketball team, and was a champion pole-vaulter.

James Dean made his film debut on a Pepsi-Cola TV commercial in which Nick Adams also appeared.

Prior to his fatal car accident in 1955 James Dean filmed a commercial for safe driving sponsored by the National Highway Committee.

Rosemary De Camp

When Rosemary De Camp appeared in *Yankee Doodle Dandy* (1942) as James Cagney's mother she was actually fourteen years younger than Cagney.

Sandra Dee

At the age of thirteen Sandra Dee was a teenage model in New York City earning $100,000 a year.

The Deep

During the filming of *The Deep* (1977) a forty-foot cruiser was sinking with three men aboard. One of the crews of the boats used for the movie raced over and saved the men from drowning.

Don Defore–Mel Ferrer

Actors Don Defore and Mel Ferrer were born on the same day, August 25, 1917.

Gloria De Haven

Bert Kalmar and Harry Ruby composed the song "Who's Sorry Now" for Flora De Haven, actress Gloria De Haven's mother. Gloria sang the song in the 1950 movie *Three Little Words* when she portrayed her own mother.

Gloria De Haven was a singer with the Bob Crosby and Jan Savitt bands.

In 1957 Gloria De Haven married Richard W. Fincher. In 1963 she divorced Fincher. In 1964 De Haven remarried Fincher. In 1968 she again divorced him. After all this, Fincher became a state senator in Florida.

Olivia de Havilland

In 1945, in a landmark decision, the Supreme Court ruled that Hollywood's long-established Anti-Peonage Law was invalid. Olivia de Havilland fought the studio system and the days of seven-year contracts were all but over.

Olivia de Havilland and Joan Fontaine

Actresses Olivia de Havilland and Joan Fontaine are sisters and were born in Tokyo, Japan, in 1916 and 1917, respectively.

Gabriel Dell

Ex-*Dead End* kid Gabriel Dell is married to Allyson Daniell, daughter of actor Henry Daniell.

Cecil B. De Mille

Cecil B. De Mille, producer of numerous religious spectaculars, was the son of a preacher.

Cecil B. De Mille filmed three versions of *The Squaw Man* (1913, 1918, 1931) and two versions of *The Ten Commandments* (1923, 1956).

In 1919 Cecil B. De Mille founded Mercury Aviation Company. Two years later the company folded.

On February 14, 1929, the very same day as the famous St. Valentine's Day Massacre in Chicago, the Brown Derby restaurant in Hollywood first opened its doors. Built in the shape of a derby hat the restaurant soon became famous, especially for the caricatures of movie stars hung on its walls. The restaurant was designed by Cecil B. De Mille.

In 1937 the Republican party nominated Cecil B. De Mille for senator from California. De Mille turned down the nomination.

Cecil B. De Mille was too busy filming the 1942 John Wayne movie *Reap the Wild Wind* to place his handprints in cement at Grauman's Chinese Theatre so Sid Grauman brought a block of wet cement to De Mille on the set. He then returned it to the front of his famous landmark.

Cecil B. De Mille was a delegate to the Republican National Convention held in Chicago in July 1952.

Many of the uniforms worn by the cadets at the United States Air Force Academy, such as the Service Alpha general purpose uniform, were designed by Cecil B. De Mille.

Richard Denning

Richard Denning played opposite Barbara Britton on the TV series *Mr. and Mrs. North.* In 1941 when Paramount Pictures gave Miss Britton her first screen test it was with Richard Denning.

John Denver

Singer John Denver's father, Henry Deutschendorf, Sr., an Air Force pilot, set a world record in a B58 Hustler in 1961 (1200 m.p.h.). He also holds two other aviation records.

The host of NBC's first *Midnight Special,* aired on August 19, 1972, was John Denver.

Bruce Dern

The father of actor Bruce Dern was a former law partner of Adlai Stevenson.

The Desperate Hours

Spencer Tracy was ready to appear in the 1955 movie *The Desperate Hours* opposite Humphrey Bogart, but an argument about the billing resulted in Fredric March taking the role.

Detective Story

Lee Grant and Joseph Wiseman both made their movie debut in *Detective Story* (1951).

Andre de Toth

The director of the 1953 3-D movie *House of Wax*, André de Toth, only had one eye and therefore could not appreciate the full effect of his movie.

The Devil and Daniel Webster

Edward Arnold replaced Thomas Mitchell as Daniel Webster in the 1940 movie *The Devil and Daniel Webster* after Mitchell broke a leg. However, RKO had already filmed several crowd scenes with Mitchell which they never bothered to reshoot. He can still be seen by alert viewers.

Andy Devine

James Ward, the grandfather of Andy Devine, was an admiral in the U.S. Navy and was a founder of the Naval Academy.

Andy Devine got his rough voice when, as a child, he was running with a curtain rod in his mouth. He fell and the rod pierced the roof of his mouth.

The late Andy Devine was once a professional football player.

Brandon de Wilde

Brandon de Wilde got one of his big breaks when Tommy Rettig turned down a role in the Broadway production of *The Member of the Wedding* (1952).

Brad Dexter

Actor Brad Dexter saved the lives of Frank Sinatra and Ruth Koch, wife of producer Howard Koch, from drowning in an undertow off a Hawaiian beach on May 10, 1964.

Dial M for Murder

Alfred Hitchcock originally filmed the 1954 movie *Dial M for Murder* in 3-D although it was never shown as such.

Angie Dickinson

Because she didn't want to go on location, Angie Dickinson turned down the role of Hot Lips Houlihan in the 1970 film *M*A*S*H*. Sally Kellerman then was cast for the part.

Marlene Dietrich

Marlene Dietrich's father, Louis Dietrich, was a winner of the Iron Cross medal during the Franco-Prussian War. He was a cavalry major.

It was Marlene Dietrich who affectionately conferred upon author Ernest Hemingway his nickname of "Papa."

113

For Marlene Dietrich's work during World War II for the Allied forces she was awarded the French Legion of Honor, the U.S. Medal of Freedom, and a Russian medal.

Bradford Dillman

Bradford Dillman's father, Joseph Dillman, was a partner in the brokerage firm of E. F. Hutton & Company.

Dino, Desi and Billy

Desi Arnaz, Jr. and Dean Martin's son Dino were members of the 1960s rock group Dino, Desi and Billy. The band was managed by Bill Howard, son of Dorothy Lamour.

Directors

Charles Laughton directed only one film, *The Night of the Hunter* (1955), which was not successful. Marlon Brando only directed one film, *One-Eyed Jacks* (1961), which also lost money.

Dirty Harry

Dirty Harry Callahan, the San Francisco cop played in the movies by Clint Eastwood, was originally meant as a starring role for Frank Sinatra, but a wrist injury prevented Sinatra from playing the part.

Walt Disney

Ernest Hemingway and Walt Disney both served as ambulance drivers in and after World War I, and both held jobs with the Kansas City *Star*. Hemingway was a reporter and Disney an artist.

Walt Disney once received four Academy Awards in a single presentation. He won for: Best Cartoon (*Toot, Whistle, Plunk and Boom*), Best Documentary Short (*The Alaskan Eskimo*), Best Documentary Feature (*The Living Desert*), and Best Two-Reel Short Subject (*Bear Country*), all in 1953.

Doctor Dolittle

While filming the 1967 movie *Doctor Dolittle* Rex Harrison was bitten by a parrot, a dog, a chimp, and a duck.

Doctor Kildare

The character Doctor Kildare was the creation of Western writer Max Brand.

Doctor Zhivago–The Ten Commandments–Moses, the Lawgiver

In the 1965 movie *Doctor Zhivago*, starring Omar Sharif as Yuri Zhivago, Sharif's own son Tarek played Zhivago at age seven. In *The Ten Commandments* (1956) Fraser Heston, son of Charlton, portrayed the infant Moses. In the 1975 TV movie *Moses, the Lawgiver*,

Moses as a young man was portrayed by Will Lancaster while Moses as an adult was portrayed by Burt Lancaster, Will's father.

Robert Donat

Robert Donat withdrew from a commitment to play the title role in *Captain Blood* (1935) and thus opened the way for Errol Flynn to become a star when Warner Bros. hired him.

Robert Donat's last line on the screen was in the 1958 movie *The Inn of the Sixth Happiness*. He stated: "We shall not see each other again, I think."

Don Juan

Although *The Jazz Singer* (1927) was the first talkie, it was the movie *Don Juan* in 1926 that first introduced sound on film. The 107-piece Philharmonic Orchestra under the direction of Herman Heller performed on the soundtrack. The music was arranged by Major Bowes of *Amateur Hour* fame.

Brian Donlevy

Brian Donlevy was a bugler in General John J. Pershing's Army, which fought Pancho Villa in Mexico.

Movie tough guy Brian Donlevy was the mayor of Malibu Beach for several years.

The Donna Reed Show

In March 1962 two of the co-stars of *The Donna Reed Show* had songs released. Shelly Fabares recorded "Johnny Angel" and Paul Petersen recorded "She Can't Find Her Keys."

Donna Douglas

TV's Elly Mae Clampett, played by Donna Douglas on *The Beverly Hillbillies,* was once a Miss New Orleans.

Helen Gahagan Douglas

Helen Gahagan Douglas starred in the first version of *She* (1935), and several years later (1950) she lost a race for the California Senate to Richard Nixon.

Kirk Douglas

Kirk Douglas was the winner of an intercollegiate wrestling championship while he attended St. Lawrence University in the late 1930s. He also served as president of several school clubs.

Melvyn Douglas

During World War II Melvyn Douglas, at age forty-two, enlisted in the U.S. Army and completed the rigorous basic training.

Mike Douglas

Talk-show host Mike Douglas was once a vocalist with Kay Kyser's Kollege of Musical Knowledge (orchestra).

Mike Douglas–Merv Griffin

Mike Douglas and Merv Griffin have both played Prince Charming. Douglas sang the role in the 1959 animated movie *Sleeping Beauty* and Griffin appeared in a television production.

Paul Douglas

Six-feet, 200-pound Paul Douglas once played professional football with the Frankford Yellow Jackets in Philadelphia and later became a well-known sports announcer in the 1930s.

William O. Douglas, Jr.

William O. Douglas, Jr., son of the former Supreme Court Justice, once played a monster on an episode of the TV series *Outer Limits*.

Dracula

In addition to Bela Lugosi, at least four other actors were considered for the title role in *Dracula* after Lon Chaney, Sr.'s death in 1930: Conrad Veidt, Ian Keith, Paul Muni, and William Courtenay. Universal released *Dracula* on St. Valentine's Day, 1931, with Dracula played by Bela Lugosi, the man who had performed the role on the stage.

Marie Dressler

Actress Marie Dressler's father was the last surviving officer of the Crimean War.

Marie Dressler was the top money-making star in 1932 and 1933. MGM thus labeled her "The World's Greatest Actress."

Bobby Driscoll

Child actor Bobby Driscoll served as both the model and the voice for Walt Disney's cartoon character Peter Pan.

Dr. Jekyll and Mr. Hyde

Robert Louis Stevenson's 1886 story *The Strange Case of Dr. Jekyll and Mr. Hyde* holds the distinction of being brought to the screen no less than fourteen times.

Dr. No

Contrary to popular belief James Bond did not debut in the 1962 movie *Dr. No* (with Sean Connery) but in a TV episode of *Climax* titled "Casino Royale" on October 21, 1954. Barry Nelson played the British agent.

Dr. Strangelove

A huge custard pie fight was cut from the final release print of the 1964 movie *Dr. Strangelove*.

Joanne Dru

Actress Joanne Dru is the sister of Peter Marshall, the emcee of the TV game show *Hollywood Squares*. Their family name is Laycock.

James Drury

James Drury was in an episode of *Decision* called "The Virginian" (aired on July 6, 1958) four years before he took the title role in the long-running TV series of the same name.

John Dukakis

John Dukakis, who played Polo in *Jaws 2* (1978), is the son of Massachusetts Governor Michael Dukakis.

Patty Duke

Prior to becoming a movie and stage actress Patty Duke did TV commercials for Ronzoni spaghetti.

Patty Duke won $32,000 on the TV quiz show *The $64,000 Challenge*.

Patty Duke had a top ten record in 1965 titled "Don't Just Stand There."

Patty Duke won both an Oscar and a Tony before the age of twenty.

Douglas Dumbrille

Character actor Douglas Dumbrille appeared in both versions of Cecil B. De Mille's *The Buccaneer* (1938 and 1958).

Irene Dunne

Irene Dunne made her acting debut in the lead role of the musical stage production *Irene*.

Irene Dunne bought the five millionth ticket at Radio City Music Hall in 1934.

Irene Dunne was to have been the female star of *Now, Voyageur* (1942), but she was replaced by Bette Davis.

Irene Dunne–Peggy Wood

In New York City in 1922 two actresses appeared in a play called *The Clinging Vine*. They were Irene Dunne and Peggy Wood. Both would later play the title role in *I Remember Mama* (Dunne in the 1948 movie, Wood on the TV series).

Jimmy Durante

Jimmy Durante's famous sign-off, "Goodnight Mrs. Calabash, wherever you are!," referred to his first wife, Jeanne Olson. Calabash was the name of a Chicago suburb that they both liked.

Deanna Durbin

Deanna Durbin was at one time considered for the part of Dorothy in *The Wizard of Oz*. Her voice was also tested but rejected for the animated Walt Disney film *Snow White and the Seven Dwarfs* (1937).

Dan Duryea

While in his senior year at Cornell University Dan Duryea became president of the university drama society. The man he succeeded was Franchot Tone.

E

Easter Parade

Gene Kelly broke an ankle and was replaced by Fred Astaire in *Easter Parade* (1948).

Clint Eastwood

Clint Eastwood's Mercedes-Benz was previously owned by Pope John Paul I who served as Pontiff for only thirty-four days in 1978.

Clint Eastwood–Burt Reynolds

In the 1950s Universal studio let the contracts of both Clint Eastwood and Burt Reynolds expire on the same day because it was felt that neither one showed any promise.

Buddy Ebsen

Christian "Buddy" Ebsen would have been the Tin Man in *The Wizard of Oz*, but he suffered a bad reaction to the aluminum dust that was part of his makeup and had to be hospitalized. The role went to Jack Haley.

Buddy Ebsen has written a Civil War play about General George McClellan titled *Champagne General*.

Nelson Eddy

Nelson Eddy was descended from President Martin Van Buren.

Nelson Eddy was once a reporter for the *Philadelphia Evening Bulletin*.

Blake Edwards

Director Blake Edwards's grandfather J. Gordon Edwards directed silent-screen star Theda Bara in more than twenty films.

Ralph Edwards

Television's *This Is Your Life* host Ralph Edwards was a welterweight boxer in college.

Vince Edwards

Vince Edwards (born Vincent Edward Zoimo) has a twin brother named Robert.

Vince Edwards received a scholarship to Ohio State in 1946 after winning the Metropolitan AAU 100-meter backstroke championship.

Richard Egan

Richard Egan was a judo instructor during World War II.

Samantha Eggar

Samantha Eggar's father, Ralph J. Eggar, served as a general in the British Army.

Anita Ekberg

Anita Ekberg was to have been the star of *Sheena, Queen of the Jungle* on television but she turned the part down, and it went to Irish McCalla.

Eloise

The comic strip *Eloise* by Kay Thompson was supposedly based on the mischievous childhood of Liza Minnelli.

"Embraceable You"

"Embraceable You" was the battle hymn of Humphrey Bogart and his third wife, Mayo Methot. His nickname for her was Sluggy.

Faye Emerson

Actress Faye Emerson became the daughter-in-law of Franklin D. Roosevelt when she married his son Elliott in 1944.

Hope Emerson

Character actress Hope Emerson was the voice of Elsie the Borden Cow on TV commercials.

Emmy Awards

Don Knotts has won more Emmy Awards than Lucille Ball. To date (1980) he has won five. Rod Serling and Mary Tyler Moore have received six. Ed Asner has received seven. Carl Reiner leads with eight Emmies for acting, writing, and producing.

Leif Erickson

Prior to becoming an actor Leif Erickson was a vocalist with the Ted Fio Rito dance band.

During his service as an aviator in World War II, Leif Erickson was shot down twice by Japanese planes and was blown off the battleship *Nevada* when an enemy bomb exploded nearby.

Dale Evans

At age fourteen, Frances Octavia Smith eloped. At fifteen she gave birth to a son. At seventeen she became a widow. Today she is known as Dale Evans or Mrs. Roy Rogers. In 1967 she was elected Mother of the Year for California.

Dale Evans was once a vocalist for Anson Week's orchestra.

Robert Evans

A young actor named Robert Evans portrayed studio boss Irving Thalberg in the 1957 movie *Man of a Thousand Faces*. Later Evans became head of Paramount studio.

Robert Evans has been married to four Hollywood beauties: Sharon Hugueney, Camilla Sparv, Ali MacGraw, and Phyllis George.

Tom Ewell

During World War II actor Tom Ewell served in the U.S. Navy and rose from seaman to lieutenant (j.g.) four years later. Prior to joining the Navy, Ewell won a state speech contest in high school.

Tom Ewell–Don Ameche

Tom Ewell and Don Ameche were classmates at the Wisconsin Law School.

The Exorcist

The actual location of the exorcism on which the 1973 film *The Exorcist* was based was in St. Louis, Missouri. That particular room at Alexian Brothers Hospital had been sealed until the building was torn down in the fall of 1978.

At one point during the filming of *The Exorcist* a mysterious fire broke out on the New York location set. The neighborhood is known as "Hell's Kitchen."

The green vomit emitted by Regan Mc-

Neil (Linda Blair) in *The Exorcist* was only a simple mixture of split pea soup and oatmeal.

Exorcist II: The Heretic

There were three different endings filmed for the 1977 movie *Exorcist II: The Heretic*.

F

Nanette Fabray

Nanette Fabray, the aunt of Shelly Fabares, began in vaudeville in 1924, making her stage debut at age five. She was billed as Baby Nanette.

Fahrenheit 451

There were no written credits for the 1967 movie *Fahrenheit 451*. They were all given orally.

Douglas Fairbanks

The father of Douglas Fairbanks, Hezekiah Charles Ulman, was the founder of the

U.S. Law Association (precursor to the American Bar Association).

Douglas Fairbanks had a mountain peak in Yosemite National Park named in his honor in 1917.

Douglas Fairbanks was the first of many movie stars to live in Beverly Hills.

Fairbanks was the first president of the Academy of Motion Picture Arts and Sciences, created in 1927.

Fairbanks wrote the screenplay for the 1927 movie *The Gaucho* under the pen name of Elton Thomas. His wife, Mary Pickford, appeared in the film.

In 1930 Douglas Fairbanks set a world's record for the longest ship-to-shore telephone conversation when he called the Sherry-Netherlands Hotel in New York City from his yacht near Honolulu, 7400 miles away.

Douglas Fairbanks–Tyrone Power

The same quotation from Hamlet is on the gravestones of both Douglas Fairbanks and Tyrone Power. It reads: "Good-night, sweet prince,/And flights of angels sing thee to thy rest!"

Douglas Fairbanks, Jr.

During World War II actor Douglas Fairbanks, Jr. was the leader of a number of commando raids in Italy. He has been awarded the Silver Star, the British Distinguished Service Cross, the French Legion of Honor, and many other citations.

Peter Falk

Columbo star Peter Falk lost his right eye to a tumor at the age of three. At twelve he was called out in a baseball game while attempting to stretch a double into a triple. He promptly removed his glass eye, handed it to the umpire and declared, "You need it more than I do."

Peter Falk was a three-letter athlete at Ossining (N.Y.) High School and was president of his class.

Peter Falk has a Master's degree in Public Administration and once served as a budget director for the state of Connecticut.

A Farewell to Arms–Casablanca

Two endings were filmed for Ernest Hemingway's *A Farewell to Arms* when it was brought to the screen in 1932. In one ending Helen Hayes died, and in the other she lived. The latter ending was chosen. *Casablanca* also had two endings filmed, one in which Paul Henreid left with Ingrid Bergman and another in which she stayed with Rick Blaine. The first ending was used.

Frances Farmer

As a young lady, actress Frances Farmer was employed as an usherette at the Paramount Theater in Seattle. She would later sign a seven-year contract with Paramount studio. She won an essay contest sponsored by *National Scholastic*. At the University of Washington she dated a young man named Chet Huntley who would one day choose journalism for a career. While still a college student she won a subscription contest for the *Voice of Action,* a Communist newspaper. The prize she accepted was a trip to Moscow.

Frances Farmer spent eight years as an inmate in a state asylum in Seattle, Washington. She not only endured it, but she prevailed even to the point of writing her candid autobiography, *Will There Really Be a Morning?,* after her release.

Charles Farrell–Ralph Bellamy

Actors Charles Farrell and Ralph Bellamy were the founders of the famed Palm Springs Racquet Club.

Glenda Farrell

Actress Glenda Farrell is the only movie star buried at West Point Cemetery. Her last husband was Dr. Henry Ross, a West Point graduate.

Mia Farrow

Frank Sinatra had his then-wife, actress Mia Farrow, replaced by Jacqueline Bisset in the 1968 film *The Detective.*

Mia Farrow, daughter of actress Maureen O'Sullivan and director John Farrow, is the mother of twin boys by Andre Previn, conductor of the London Symphonic Orchestra. The boys were born on February 26, 1970.

Fathers-in-law

Producer David O. Selznick's father-in-law was Louis B. Mayer. Director Mervyn Leroy's father-in-law was producer Harry Warner. Anthony Quinn's father-in-law was Cecil B. DeMille. TV producer William T. Orr's father-in-law was Jack Warner.

Farrah Fawcett

Farrah Fawcett was arrested twice for shoplifting when she was an aspiring young actress. The first time was August 24, 1970, and the second was November 24, 1970 (the same day she received her sentence for the first arrest). In both cases she pleaded guilty to trespassing.

William Fawcett

Character actor William Fawcett, who held a Ph.D. in English literature, once taught at Michigan State.

Barbara Feldon

Barbara Feldon won the top prize on the TV quiz show *The $64,000 Question* on the subject of Shakespeare.

Jose Ferrer

José Ferrer entered Princeton University at the age of fifteen and is the recipient of honorary degrees from five universities. On radio he played detective Philo Vance.

In 1954, then husband and wife José Ferrer and Rosemary Clooney recorded the song "Man and Woman."

Mel Ferrer

Mel Ferrer's father was José Ferrer, a Cuban doctor. He was not related to the actor José Ferrer.

Mel Ferrer married Frances Pilchard, divorced her, remarried her, and again divorced her. In between his marriages to Pilchard he married and divorced Barbara Tripps. All this was prior to his marriage to Audrey Hepburn.

Stepin Fetchit

Stepin Fetchit's real name was Lincoln Theodore Monroe Andrew Perry, after four Presidents. He adopted his stage name from the name of a race horse that once won him some money.

Betty Field

Actress Betty Field is a descendant of John Alden and Priscilla Mullins, the pair of pilgrims on whom H. W. Longfellow based his famous poem *The Courtship of Miles Standish* (1858).

Sally Field

Sally Field is the step-daughter of actor Jock Mahoney.

W. C. Fields

Although sponsored by Lucky Strike cigarettes on radio, comedian W. C. Fields often referred to a nonexistent son, Chester Fields.

W. C. Fields–Charlie Chaplin

Classic comedians W. C. Fields and Charlie Chaplin both died on Christmas Day, 1946 and 1977 respectively.

W. C. Fields–Ed Wynn

W. C. Fields and Ed Wynn were both considered for the part of the Wizard in *The Wizard of Ox*. Wallace Beery wanted the role and tested for it, but the part went to Frank Morgan.

The Fighting 69th

The only female player in the 1940 James Cagney movie *The Fighting 69th* was Germaine, a mule. She won an award as the Animal Actor of the Year. The award was presented by Humphrey Bogart.

Fire Down Below

In the 1957 movie *Fire Down Below* the musical score was composed by Jack Lemmon who co-starred in the film with Robert Mitchum.

A Fistful of Dollars

Prior to Clint Eastwood accepting the starring role in his first spaghetti Western, *A Fistful of Dollars* (filmed in 1964, released in U.S. in 1967), the lead was offered to but turned down by Charles Bronson.

Geraldine Fitzgerald

Dublin-born actress Geraldine Fitzgerald is a distant relative of author James Joyce. Her father's firm, D & T Fitzgerald, is mentioned in Joyce's classic work *Ulysses*.

Pat Flaherty

Character actor Pat Flaherty was a veteran of four wars: the Mexican Border Campaign of 1916, World War I, World War II, and the Korean War.

Richard Fleischer

Richard Fleischer, director of the 1954 movie *20,000 Leagues Under the Sea*, is the son of cartoonist Max Fleischer (creator of Betty Boop).

Art Fleming

Former *Jeopardy* host Art Fleming was once a stand-in for Ralph Bellamy on the TV series *Man Against Crime*. Today Fleming is a radio talk-show host at KMOX in St. Louis.

Rhonda Fleming–Dorothy Malone

In high school Rhonda Fleming was the captain of the female basketball team. Dorothy Malone served in the same capacity at her high school.

Victor Fleming

Victor Fleming took over for George Cukor who was fired from *Gone With The Wind* (1939). Cukor then took over for Ernst Lubitsch who was fired from *The Women* (1939), while Lubitsch went on to complete *Ninotchka* (1939).

Louise Fletcher

The parents of Louise Fletcher, winner of the 1975 Best Actress Award for *One Flew Over the Cuckoo's Nest,* are both deaf. She thanked them in sign language at the presentation.

Flipper

Ricou Browning and Ben Chapman, both of whom played the Gill-Man in the movies, were closely associated with the television series *Flipper*. Chapman was production supervisor and Browning was co-creator (with Jack Cowden).

Errol Flynn

Actor Errol Flynn's father was a noted biologist whose accomplishments in Tasmania are listed in the British *Who's Who*. He was also honored with an MBE (Member of British Empire).

Errol Flynn's mother was a descendant of one of the crew members of the *Bounty*, a midshipman named Young. Flynn owned one of the swords that originally belonged to Fletcher Christian. Flynn was the first actor to play Christian in the movies. He played in a 1933 Australian version titled *In the Wake of the Bounty* (Mayne Lynton portrayed Captain Bligh).

The slang expression "In like Flynn" originated as a tribute to Errol Flynn after his famous 1942 trial in which he was acquitted of statutory rape involving two teenage girls.

Flynn won $32,000 when he made an appearance on the TV quiz program *The $64,000 Question*.

Flynn claimed in his autobiography, *My Wicked, Wicked Ways*, to have fought alongside Fidel Castro and his forces in Cuba in 1959.

Errol Flynn–Alan Hale

Actors Errol Flynn and Alan Hale appeared in twelve movies together.

Errol Flynn–Sterling Hayden

Both Errol Flynn and Sterling Hayden had best-selling books about sea adventures. Flynn wrote *Beams Ends* in 1937 and *Showdown* in 1946. Hayden wrote *Wanderer* in 1963 and *Voyage* in 1976.

Errol Flynn–Merle Oberon

Errol Flynn and Merle Oberon were both born in Tasmania.

Henry Fonda

Henry Fonda was cast in his first film role because Gary Cooper and Joel McCrea were unavailable to do *The Farmer Takes a Wife* in 1935.

In the 1964 movie *The Best Man* Henry Fonda played presidential candidate William Russell. In Fonda's very next movie, *Fail Safe* (1964), he played the President of the United States.

Henry Fonda has had some of his paintings displayed in art galleries and exhibitions and has been commissioned to do some paintings for greeting cards.

Jane Fonda

Jane Fonda was the first member of her acting family to win an Oscar. She won for Best Actress in 1971 for *Klute* and again in 1978 for *Coming Home*.

Jane Fonda was an early choice to play Chris McNeil in *The Exorcist* (1973). The part went to Ellen Burstyn.

Joan Fontaine–Olivia de Havilland

When Joan Fontaine won an Oscar as Best Actress for the 1941 movie *Suspicion,* one of the other nominees was her sister, Olivia de Havilland. Miss de Havilland had been nominated for her role in *Hold Back the Dawn* (1941).

Sisters Joan Fontaine and Olivia de Havilland both have I.Q.s in the genius range.

Lillian Fontaine

Lillian Fontaine, the mother of Joan Fontaine and Olivia de Havilland, made her acting debut in the 1945 movie *The Lost Weekend.*

Glenn Ford

Sir John MacDonald, a former prime minister of Canada, was the uncle of actor Glenn Ford.

Glenn Ford is a descendant of President Martin Van Buren.

In his youth Glenn Ford was a stable boy for humorist Will Rogers.

During World War II Ford was the director of the camera team that documented German atrocities at the concentration camp Dachau.

Glen Ford is a captain in the U.S. Naval Reserves. He served in Vietnam during the mid-1960s as commander of a Marine battalion and was twice shot down in a helicopter.

John Ford

Director John Ford was on Midway Island on June 4, 1942, when the Japanese attacked. In the air attack he received a grazing wound to his left forearm.

John Ford was awarded four Oscars as Best Director. The movies were: *The Informer* (1935), *The Grapes of Wrath* (1940), *How*

Green Was My Valley (1941), and *The Quiet Man* (1952). Although he won more Oscars than any other director, none of them were for any of his great Westerns.

In April 1973, John Ford was given the first Life Achievement Award by the American Film Institute. At the Hollywood ceremony President Richard Nixon conferred on him both the Presidential Medal of Freedom and a promotion to Admiral.

John Ford–Raoul Walsh

Directors John Ford and Raoul Walsh both wore eye patches (Ford on his right eye, Walsh on his left).

John Forsythe

John Forsythe, the voice of Charlie on the TV series *Charlie's Angels,* once served as a public-address announcer at Ebbets Field in New York.

Redd Foxx

In his youth, comedian Redd Foxx was a close friend of Malcolm Little (later known as Malcolm X) in New York City. Foxx became known as "Chicago Red," while Malcolm Little became known as "Detroit Red." Foxx later belonged to a singing trio called the Bon-Bons who won second prize on Major Bowes's *Amateur Hour.*

Redd Foxx's real name is John Elroy Sanford. His brother and father were both named

Fred Sanford, the role he played on the series *Sanford and Son.*

Arlene Francis

Long-time *What's My Line?* panelist Arlene Francis played a prostitute in the 1932 movie *Murders in the Rue Morgue.* In the movie she was rejected by Bela Lugosi.

Francis the Talking Mule

In the Universal movie series about Francis the Talking Mule, the voice of Francis in the first six films was provided by Chill Wills. The seventh and last movie had Paul Frees as the voice of Francis.

John Frankenheimer

Director John Frankenheimer made a cameo appearance as a TV director in the Collesium control room in his 1977 film *Black Sunday.*

Frankenstein

The 1931 movie *Frankenstein* was actually filmed with a green tint. This was done to emphasize the Monster's features.

It wasn't until after *Frankenstein* had been released that it was revealed just who had played the Monster. It was, of course, Boris Karloff (born William Henry Pratt).

Boris Karloff did not play Frankenstein in the 1931 movie of that title. He was credited as

"The Monster." Colin Clive played Dr. Henry Frankenstein.

Mona Freeman

Howard Hughes signed Mona Freeman to a movie contract when he saw her picture on the cover of a popular magazine.

Paul Frees

Paul Frees, a distinguished radio actor, has found greater financial reward but less recognition in television. His voice has been used for the following TV characters: Professor Ludwig von Drake, Heckle and Jeckle, Inspector Ray Fenwick on *Dudley Do-Right,* Boris Badenov on *Rocky and his Friends,* and, although he was never billed for it, John Beresford Tipton on the TV series *The Millionaire.*

The French Connection

Gene Hackman got the part of Jimmy "Popeye" Doyle in the 1971 film *The French Connection* although Jackie Gleason and columnist Jimmy Breslin were both seriously considered.

From Here to Eternity

Studio chief Harry Cohn wanted Eli Wallach to play Angelo Maggio in the 1953 film *From Here to Eternity.* Frank Sinatra was the final choice, picking up a Best Supporting Actor Oscar for his efforts. Cohn wanted Aldo Ray to play Prewitt in the same film but Fred Zinnemann refused to direct the picture unless Montgomery Clift got the part.

The Front

The 1976 Woody Allen movie *The Front* was written by, directed by, and featured actors who were all blacklisted in the 1950s, including Zero Mostel and Herschel Bernardi.

G

Clark Gable

When Clark Gable was born on February 1, 1901, in Cadiz, Ohio, he was mistakenly listed as a female on his birth certificate.

Clark Gable originally billed himself as Clarke Gabel, changing the spelling in both names. His real name was William Clark Gable.

Clark Gable's first wife, Josephine Dillon, was fourteen years his senior. His second wife, Rhea Langham, was eleven years his senior.

For Clark Gable's first screen test he was required to wear South Sea garb and had a hibiscus behind his ear. No wonder he failed the test.

Clark Gable once won a gold medal by

hitting 49 out of 50 targets in a skeet tournament.

German Luftwaffe Commander Hermann Goering had a bounty of $5000 on Clark Gable dead or alive during World War II. The lucky pilot who could down Gable would also have received a promotion and a leave of absence.

Carole Lombard, Loretta Young, Jeanette MacDonald, Vivien Leigh, Greta Garbo, Ava Gardner, Lana Turner, Jean Harlow, Greer Garson, Joan Crawford, Barbara Stanwyck, Norma Shearer, Myrna Loy, Claudette Colbert, Hedy Lamarr, Marilyn Monroe, Mary Astor, Yvonne De Carlo, Sophia Loren, Rosalind Russell, Deborah Kerr, Susan Hayward, Gene Tierney, and Doris Day all starred opposite Hollywood's King, Clark Gable.

Clark Gable wore false teeth throughout most of his film career, one of Hollywood's best-kept secrets. Humphrey Bogart, Sean Connery, Burt Reynolds, and John Wayne have all worn toupees.

Clark Gable–Humphrey Bogart

Clark Gable, who was married five times, and Humphrey Bogart, who was married four times, both had first wives who were older than themselves.

Clark Gable–Charles Bronson–Sabu

Clark Gable, Charles Bronson, and Sabu all served as aerial gunners in bombers during their tour of duty with the military in World War II.

Clark Gable–Jean Harlow

Fox studios once turned down both Clark Gable and Jean Harlow in screen tests.

Clark Gable–Myrna Loy

In 1938 Ed Sullivan presented King and Queen of Hollywood crowns to Clark Gable and Myrna Loy over NBC radio. Spencer Tracy had already crowned Gable "the King" at the MGM commissary with a studio prop earlier that year. Sullivan polled the readers of his syndicated newspaper column to determine the winners.

Clark Gable–Tyrone Power

Clark Gable and Tyrone Power (both Ohio-born) became fathers of first sons after each great actor had passed away.

Zsa Zsa Gabor

Zsa Zsa Gabor won the title of Miss Hungary in 1936, but had to give up the honor when it was revealed that she was not yet sixteen years old, the minimum age.

Zsa Zsa Gabor's sixth husband, Jack Ryan, whom she divorced in August 1976, was the manufacturer of the Barbie Doll.

The Gallant Hours

In the 1960 movie *The Gallant Hours*, directed by Robert Montgomery and starring

James Cagney, both Robert Montgomery, Jr.,
and James Cagney; Jr., played U.S. soldiers.

Greta Garbo

Film actress Greta Garbo refused to appear on radio. In 1934 she turned down a
$25,000 offer for a single guest appearance. She
was Adolf Hitler's favorite actress.

Greta Garbo—Eddie "Rochester" Anderson

Greta Garbo and actor Eddie "Rochester"
Anderson were both born on September 18,1905.

Greta Garbo—Grace Kelly

Foreign stamps have been issued honoring
Greta Garbo and Grace Kelly. Walt Disney has
been honored with a U.S. stamp.

Erle Stanley Gardner

The creator of Perry Mason, author Erle
Stanley Gardner, made an appearance in the
last episode of TV's *Perry Mason* series in 1966.
The title was "The Case of the Final Fade-
Out."

John Garfield

Director Elia Kazan first offered the role of
Stanley Kowalski in *A Streetcar Named Desire*
(1951) to John Garfield. Marlon Brando got
the part when Garfield refused it because he

148

felt the role was secondary to the character of Blanche.

Julie Garfield, the daughter of John Garfield, appeared in the 1970 movie *Love Story*.

William Gargan

William Gargan, one of many actors to play detective Ellery Queen, was himself a detective before becoming an actor.

William Gargan, who in 1960 played a cancer-stricken U.S. President in the play *The Best Man*, died of cancer eighteen years later.

Judy Garland

Hugh Fitzpatrick, Judy Garland's great-grandfather, was Ulysses S. Grant's first cousin.

According to legend, when George Jessel introduced child singer Frances Gumm for the first time he momentarily forgot her real name and introduced her as Judy Garland because he had just sent actress Judith Anderson a note using the word garland. The name just popped into his head. Thereafter Frances Gumm was known as Judy Garland. Another story credits Les Brown as giving her the name after he saw her playing The Lodge at Lake Tahoe.

At Clark Gable's thirty-sixth birthday party Judy Garland sang "Dear Mr. Gable" to the tune of "You Made Me Love You." Louis B. Mayer was so impressed with the performance that he included it in the 1937 movie *Broadway Melody of 1938*.

Judy Garland sang the last eight bars of "Over the Rainbow" several times to President John Kennedy over the telephone at his request.

On the day of Judy Garland's death, June 23, 1969, a tornado touched down in Kansas.

On May 3, 1970, MGM auctioned off Judy Garland's size 4½ ruby red slippers from *The Wizard of Oz* for $15,000.

Judy Garland–Jason Robards, Jr.

Judy Garland and Jason Robards, Jr., graduated in the same 1937 class at Bancroft Junior High School in Los Angeles.

James Garner

James Garner, who was the first man drafted from the state of Oklahoma in the Korean War, was once so far behind enemy lines that he was wounded by friendly fire.

James Garner's brother Jack was a pitcher for the Pittsburgh Pirates.

Greer Garson

Greer Garson holds the record for a "Thank You" speech after accepting her Oscar as Best Actress of 1942 for the film *Mrs. Miniver*. She thanked the crowd on March 4, 1943, for nearly ten minutes.

John Gavin

In 1961 John Gavin was appointed special advisor to Secretary General José Mora of the

OAS (Organization of American States). He has been awarded the Order of Balboa by the Panamanian government and the Order of the Eloy Alfaro Foundation of Ecuador.

Janet Gaynor

Janet Gaynor is an accomplished painter whose works have been on exhibit. Her canvasses have sold for upward of $2000 apiece.

Will Geer

Will Geer held a master's degree in botany from Columbia University. His hobby was raising all the plants mentioned in the works of Shakespeare.

The George Raft Story

Dean Martin and Tony Curtis were both considered for the title role in *The George Raft Story* (1961) before the part went to Ray Danton.

Gerber baby

Humphrey Bogart was *not* the baby used by Gerber Baby Food. However, one of his mother's illustrations of him was used by Mellins Baby Food. Ann Turner Cook was the baby used in 1928 to pose for the famous picture of the Gerber baby. Dorothy Hope Smith did the illustrations. Mitzi Gaynor's real name is Francesca Mitzi Gerber.

Hoot Gibson

Edward Gibson received his nickname "Hoot" from his hobby of hunting owls in Nebraska.

In 1912 Hoot Gibson won the All-Around Champion Cowboy title at the Pendleton Roundup.

In 1933, Western star Hoot Gibson was seriously injured in an airplane crash in the National Air Races held in Los Angeles. He was racing in a special match against another Western star, Ken Maynard.

Helen Gilbert

An MGM starlet, Helen Gilbert, had the role of Glinda the Good Witch in *The Wizard of Oz* promised to her, but she chose instead to run off with Howard Hughes. The part went to Billie Burke.

Paul Michael Glaser

Paul Michael Glaser (Dave Starsky on *Starsky and Hutch*) was formerly a regular member of the casts on the TV soaps *Love of Life* and *Love Is a Many Splendored Thing*.

Jackie Gleason

At the age of twenty Jackie Gleason became a daredevil race-car driver for a short time.

In the city of Miami Beach there is a street named Jackie Gleason Drive.

Paulette Goddard

During World War II actress Paulette Goddard became the first civilian woman to fly over the Himalaya mountains.

The Godfather

The head of the racehorse, Khartoum, in the 1972 movie *The Godfather* was not a prop; it was an actual horse's head.

The Godfather—Gone With The Wind

The word "Mafia" is conspicuously missing from the movie *The Godfather*. Mafia is an acronym for *Morte Alla Francia Italia Anela* (Death to the French is Italy's Cry). Due to protests from the Italian-American League the word was omitted, yet it was used in the 1974 sequel, *The Godfather, Part II*. Because of protests from the NAACP (National Association for the Advancement of Colored People) the word "nigger" was omitted from the 1939 movie *Gone With The Wind*.

The Godfather, Part II

In the 1974 movie *The Godfather, Part II* Henry Kaiser's former estate at Lake Tahoe, Nevada, was used for film location of the Corleone estate.

Arthur Godfrey

In the 1948 presidential election Arthur Godfrey received four write-in votes from the state of Alabama.

Arthur Godfrey is second only to Lucille Ball for having his picture appear the most often on the cover of *TV Guide*.

Going My Way

Bing Crosby won an Oscar as Best Actor for the 1944 movie *Going My Way*. Barry Fitzgerald won a Best Supporting Actor Oscar for the same movie. Fitzgerald had been nominated in both the Best Actor and the Best Supporting Actor categories for the film. This was the first and, to date, the only time that an actor has been nominated in two separate categories for the same picture.

Gold Diggers of 1933

In the movie *Gold Diggers of 1933* Ginger Rogers sang "We're in the Money" in pig Latin on a whim. This scene was later shown in the 1967 movie *Bonnie and Clyde*.

Golden Boy

Harry Cohn wanted John Garfield for the 1939 film *Golden Boy*, but Warner Bros. refused to loan out Garfield and the movie was made with William Holden, the actor that director Rouben Mamoulian wanted. Ironically

Golden Boy would later be Garfield's last stage appearance. He died in 1952, ten months after the play opened.

Samuel Goldwyn

Samuel Goldwyn had a reputation for unpredictable decisions. During his reign as a studio boss he turned down people like Clark Gable, Gary Cooper, Bette Davis, Greta Garbo, and Robert Montgomery.

Samuel Goldwyn never carried anything in his pockets, even a wallet, so that his clothing would always have smooth, flowing lines.

Gone With The Wind

The original title for the novel *Gone With The Wind* was to have been *Tomorrow Is Another Day*. Scarlett was to have been Pansy O'Hara and the plantation Tara was to be called Fontenoy Hall.

The burning of Atlanta, Georgia, the first scene filmed in *Gone With The Wind*, employed the old RKO *King Kong* set for the impressive sequence.

Elizabeth Taylor might have played the child, Bonnie Blue, in *Gone With The Wind* at age seven, but her father said she was too young to appear in films. The part went to Cammie King.

The trees shown in front of the plantation Tara in *Gone With The Wind* were made of plaster. Real leaves had to be attached to the

155

phony trees. There were 1,250,000 props used in the movie.

The horse that Gerald O'Hara (Thomas Mitchell) rode in *Gone With The Wind* was the Silver of Lone Ranger serial fame.

Rhett Butler's famous closing line was actually filmed two ways. "Frankly, my dear, I don't care" was not used.

On the day that *Gone With The Wind* premiered in Atlanta, Georgia (December 15, 1939) the state's governor declared the day an official state holiday.

Six actors who appeared in *Gone With The Wind* went on to star in their own TV series. They were: George Reeves (*Superman*), Hattie McDaniel (*Beulah*), Thomas Mitchell (*O. Henry Playhouse*), Cliff Edwards (*Ukulele Ike*), Victor Jory (*Manhunt*), and Ward Bond (*Wagon Train*). Others from the cast who appeared in TV series were Rand Brooks, Eddie Anderson, and Butterfly McQueen.

A *musical* version of *Gone With The Wind* debuted on January 2, 1970, in Tokyo, Japan, at the Imperial Theatre. Sakura Jingui played Scarlett in the four-hour production. An English version then opened at the Drury Lane Theatre in London on May 3, 1972, with June Ritchie as Scarlett.

Goodbye Columbus

The 1969 movie Goodbye Columbus, based on the Philip Roth novel, was the motion picture debut of Richard Benjamin and Ali MacGraw.

Bernard Gorcey

The father of *Bowery Boys* star Leo Gorcey, Bernard Gorcey, was the first actor to play the leading role of Isaac Cohen in Anne Nichols's play *Abie's Irish Rose* (1922) which played on Broadway for 2,327 performances.

Gale Gordon

Comic foil Gale Gordon was the voice of Flash Gordon on radio.

Ruth Gordon

Actress Ruth Gordon has co-authored three screenplays with her writer/husband Garson Kanin that have been nominated for Academy Awards. They were *A Double Life* (1948), *Adam's Rib* (1949), and *Pat and Mike* (1952).

Frank Gorshin

Frank Gorshin once bought an old violin at a Reno, Nevada flea market, paying $15.00 for the instrument. The "old violin" turned out to be a Stradivarius.

Marjoe Gortner

Marjoe Gortner, one-time child evangelist and now an actor, performed his first marriage ceremony at the age of four (January 4, 1949).

Robert Goulet

Many people are convinced that Robert Goulet is Canadian by birth, due to the fact that Ed Sullivan introduced him as such on his show many times. Actually Goulet was born in Massachusetts.

Robert Goulet's first job was as a disc jockey and radio announcer with station CKCA in Edmonton, Canada.

Betty Grable

Betty Grable (born Elizabeth Grable) had her name changed in films to Frances Dean by Samuel Goldwyn until he let her go as an unlikely star. She was once a vocalist with Jay Whidden's orchestra.

Although she starred in the 1939 movie *Million Dollar Legs*, Betty Grable's legs were actually insured for "only" $250,000.

Betty Grable–Veronica Lake

Two of Hollywood's most famous pin-up queens, Betty Grable and Veronica Lake, died within five days of each other in July 1973.

The Graduate

The original choice for the part of Mrs. Robinson in the 1967 movie *The Graduate* was French actress Jeanne Moreau. The role went to Anne Bancroft.

Dustin Hoffman received only $17,000 for his starring role of Benjamin Braddock in *The*

Graduate. After the movie he collected unemployment insurance. The film grossed over $50,000 million.

Gloria Grahame

Gloria Grahame married Nicholas Ray in 1948 and divorced him in 1952. She then married Cy Howard (1954-57). In 1961 she returned to the Ray family by marrying Nicholas's son Tony. Since she had a son, Timothy, by Nicholas this not only made Timothy Tony's stepbrother but also his stepson.

Stewart Granger

Stewart Granger had to change his name. Reason: his real name is James Stewart.

In 1964 Stewart Granger married twenty-two-year-old Caroline Lecerf, Miss Belgium of 1962. David Niven was best man.

Cary Grant

Cary Grant's second wife, Barbara Hutton, was once called the World's Wealthiest Woman. She was the heiress to the Woolworth fortune.

Cary Grant claimed that while filming the 1959 movie *North by Northwest* he was cured of his acrophobia (fear of heights).

Cary Grant–James Cagney

Cary Grant never said "Judy Judy Judy" in any of his films, nor did James Cagney ever say "You dirty rat" in any of his films.

Cary Grant–Gregory Peck

On the afternoon of June 27, 1978, Cary Grant and Gregory Peck ran their automobiles into each other while arriving at David Niven's home. The gathering was a pre-nuptial party for Princess Caroline of Monaco and her husband-to-be, Philippe Junot.

Gogi Grant

Gogi Grant sang for Ann Blyth in her portrayal of torch singer Helen Morgan in the 1957 movie *The Helen Morgan Story*.

Grauman's Chinese Theatre

According to Hollywood legend, the first person to leave prints in the cement outside Grauman's Chinese Theatre was Norma Talmadge when on May 18, 1927, she accidentally stepped into newly laid cement. Publicity did the rest, and a tradition was born.

Grease

Henry Winkler and Susan Dey both turned down the lead roles in the movie version of the Broadway play *Grease*.

The Great Escape

Charles Bronson, whose character in *The Great Escape* (1963) experienced claustrophobia while digging an escape tunnel, once worked in the coal mines of Pennsylvania digging coal for $1.00 a ton.

The Great Gatsby

Actor Howard Da Silva appeared in both the 1949 and 1974 versions of *The Great Gatsby*.

In the 1974 version of *The Great Gatsby*, starring Robert Redford and Mia Farrow, the house used for Jay Gatsby's home was actually named Rosecliff and was designed by famed architect Stanford White, whose life was depicted in the 1955 movie *The Girl in the Red Velvet Swing*.

The Great Race

In *The Great Race* (1965), Professor Fate's (Jack Lemmon) automobile was the Hannibal Twin 8. There were actually six different cars built for the movie, each performing a separate function.

The Great Ziegfeld

In *The Great Ziegfeld* (1936), Dennis Morgan's singing voice was dubbed by Allan Jones, the father of singer Jack Jones.

Lorne Greene

Ottawa-born actor Lorne Greene was the 1965 recipient of the highly honored title of Canada's Man of the Year.

Sydney Greenstreet

Sydney Greenstreet was sixty-one when he made his screen debut in *The Maltese Falcon* (1941).

Jane Greer

The first WAC uniform was modeled by Jane Greer in *Life* magazine in 1942. The photo came to the attention of a Hollywood producer, eventually allowing her to become a successful actress. She has a twin brother named Donne.

Merv Griffin–Andrew Sisters

Merv Griffin, while under contract to Freddy Martin in 1951, recorded the song "I've Got a Lovely Bunch of Coconuts." Record sales were three million but Griffin was paid only $50.00 for his singing. Likewise, the Andrews Sisters received only $50.00 for their rendition of "Bel Mir Bist du Schoen," a song which sold over a million copies.

Andy Griffith–Dan Blocker

Andy Griffith and Dan Blocker were both schoolteachers prior to becoming actors.

D. W. Griffith

D. W. Griffith was an innovator in the early years of motion pictures, producing and directing almost 500 movies. He was the first director to make a film longer than 1000 feet. On one occasion, when he ordered the first close-up of a human face the cameraman refused and quit in disgust.

David Groh

TV actor David Groh attended the London Academy of Music and Dramatic Art on a Fulbright Scholarship.

Alec Guinness

In his youth Alec Guinness was a short distance runner, winning many trophies for his skills.

Gunsmoke

Raymond Burr, John Wayne, and William Conrad were all considered for the part of Matt Dillon on TV's *Gunsmoke*. Conrad had first essayed the role on radio. When John Wayne turned down the part of Matt Dillon he suggested James Arness, an actor he had worked with in a few films, for the part. The first episode of *Gunsmoke* was introduced by John Wayne. Arness did not initially want the role, but after twenty years it meant about $20,000,-000 to him.

Guys and Dolls

Gene Kelly, Gary Grant, and Burt Lancaster were all considered for the part of Sky Masterson in the 1955 movie *Guys and Dolls*. The part went to Marlon Brando.

H

Gene Hackman

Gene Hackman, who joined the U.S. Marine Corps at age sixteen, was demoted on three different occasions.

In one year Gene Hackman won four major acting awards: a Golden Globe, a New York Film Critics Award, a National Association of Theater Owners "Star of the Year" Award, and an Oscar. They were for his performance in *The French Connection* (1971).

Jean Hagen–Patricia Neal

Jean Hagen and Patricia Neal were roommates at Northwestern University before either chose to go into acting.

Dan Haggerty

Actor and animal trainer Dan Haggerty was the builder of one of the custom motorcycles that appeared in the 1969 movie *Easy Rider*.

Larry Hagman–James MacArthur

The mothers of TV personalities Larry Hagman and James MacArthur are both first ladies of the theater. Hagman's mother is Mary Martin. MacArthur's stepmother is Helen Hayes.

Alan Hale

Alan Hale had many jobs before he became a great character actor. He wrote obituaries, studied osteopathy, and sang with the Metropolitan Opera Company of New York.

Jon Hall

Jon Hall, who became famous on TV as *Ramar of the Jungle*, was tested by Universal for the role of Flash Gordon, a role that went to Larry "Buster" Crabbe.

Billy Halop

Billy Halop, who was once a member of the Dead End Kids, later became a male nurse.

Mark Hamill

Mark Hamill played on the TV soap *General Hospital* from 1972 to 1973 as Nurse Brewer's nephew.

Margaret Hamilton

Edna May Oliver and Gale Sondergaard were both considered for the Wicked Witch of the West, in *The Wizard of Oz*. The part went to Margaret Hamilton, a former kindergarten teacher.

Neil Hamilton

Neil Hamilton appeared in magazine and newspaper ads of the 1920s as the Arrow Collar Man.

Dashiell Hammett

Dashiell Hammett, creator of the Thin Man and Sam Spade, was himself a Pinkerton detective for eight years.

Ty Hardin

Western actor Ty Hardin is today a practicing minister in Prescott, Arizona.

Ann Harding

Actress Ann Harding, born Dorothy Walton Gatley, is the daughter of George C. Gatley, a Brigadier Army General and a West Point graduate.

Cedric Hardwicke

Cedric Hardwicke was a captain in the Judge Advocate's branch of the British Army during World War I.

Cedric Hardwicke–Jean Harlow

The fathers of Cedric Hardwicke and Jean Harlow were both doctors.

Andy Hardy

The house used in the famous MGM movie series about the life of Andy Hardy (Mickey Rooney) was later used for the home and office of Dr. Marcus Welby (Robert Young) on television.

Oliver Hardy

Oliver Hardy opened the first motion picture house in the town of Milledgeville, Georgia, in 1910.

Jean Harlow

Jean Harlow was the first actress to appear on the cover of *Life* magazine (May 3, 1937).

Jean Harlow–Marilyn Monroe

Both Jean Harlow (*Saratoga*, 1937) and Marilyn Monroe (*The Misfits*, 1961) co-starred with Clark Gable in their last movies. Harlow did not complete hers. Mary Dees stood in for her, and Paula Winslowe dubbed her voice.

Julie Harris

Director Fred Zinnemann wanted Julie Harris for the part of Alma in *From Here to Eternity* (1953) but the role went to Donna Reed who won the Best Supporting Actress Award for her efforts.

Richard Harris

Richard Harris had a number one record in 1968, "MacArthur Park."

Linda Harrison

Linda Harrison, who played the mute girl Nova in *Planet of the Apes* (1968), once held the title Miss Maryland and was a contestant in the Miss Universe pageant.

Noel Harrison

Rex Harrison's son Noel was on the British Olympic ski team in the 1952 and 1956 Olympics.

Rex Harrison

Rex Harrison was given the nickname "Sexy Rexy" by columnist Hedda Hopper. He has only one eye, the other is made of glass.

In the making of *Cleopatra* (1963) Rex

Harrison had a clause in his contract stipulating that whenever Richard Burton's picture appeared on an ad so would his. A large sign was put up on Broadway showing Burton and Elizabeth Taylor. After Harrison's lawyers complained, the studio had a small picture (a very small picture) of Harrison placed in a corner of the billboard.

Even though he had played the part of Henry Higgins on the stage, Rex Harrison was not the first actor considered for the movie *My Fair Lady* (1964). Cary Grant and Peter O'Toole refused the part in deference to Harrison.

Dolores Hart

Dolores Hart, the actress who appeared in such films as *Loving You* (1957) and *Wild Is the Wind* (1957), gave up acting in the 1960s to become a nun. She lives in the convent of Regina Laudis in Bethlehem, Connecticut.

William S. Hart

Silent Western hero William S. Hart posed for the original Uncle Sam recruiting poster of World War I.

David Hartman

David Hartman, who played a retired baseball player on the TV series *Lucas Tanner*, was actually offered contracts to play for the Philadelphia Phillies and the Boston Braves.

Laurence Harvey

Laurence Harvey was a member of the Royal South African Navy.

Have Gun Will Travel–My Little Margie–I Love Lucy

The only three radio series to become spin-offs from a TV program are *Have Gun Will Travel*, *My Little Margie*, and *I Love Lucy*. *Gun*, starring Richard Boone, ran on television from 1957 to 1963. The radio series, starring John Dehner, ran from 1958 to 1960. *Margie* debuted on TV on June 23, 1952, and became a radio show on December 7, 1952. *Lucy* started on TV in 1951, and the radio version appeared in 1952, its only year.

June Haver

At the age of six June Haver played piano with the Cincinnati Symphony Orchestra. At ten she starred in a radio script that she herself wrote and directed. While in high school she was the winner of several oratory contests. She later became the female vocalist with the Dick Jurgens, Freddy Martin, Ted Fio Rito, and Tommy Dorsey orchestras.

June Havoc

As a child June Havoc, the younger sister of Gypsy Rose Lee, was billed as Dainty Baby Jane. She was married at thirteen and was a mother at sixteen. She danced in a marathon which lasted four months, coming in second with her partner and splitting $100.00 for 3000 hours of dancing. She later sang with a few orchestras.

June Havoc is the owner of the Civil War town of Cannon Crossing in Connecticut.

Howard Hawks

In 1914 future director Howard Hawks won the U.S. Junior Tennis Championship at the age of eighteen.

Howard Hawks was a professional race car driver in his youth. He helped design the winning car in the 1936 Indy 500.

Sessue Hayakawa

Actor Sessue Hayakawa was a Buddhist priest. His father was a governor of Chiba Prefecture in Japan.

Sterling Hayden

Sterling Hayden was a member of the OSS during World War II and held an officer's rank. He went on several missions behind the German lines.

From June to December 1946 Sterling Hayden was a self-confessed member of the Communist party.

Helen Hayes

When Helen Hayes saw the first movie in which she appeared, *The Sin of Madelon*

Claudet (1931), she was so shocked by her performance that she attempted to buy the movie from the studio so that she could destroy it. She won an Oscar for Best Actress for her role in the movie.

Louis Hayward–Basil Rathbone–John Charles Daly

Actors Louis Hayward and Basil Rathbone were both born in Johannesburg, South Africa. John Charles Daly, long-time moderator of *What's My Line?*, was also born there.

Susan Hayward

Susan Hayward was discovered by George Cukor when he saw her face on the cover of the *Saturday Evening Post*.

In three films Susan Hayward played an alcoholic: *Smash Up* (1947), *My Foolish Heart* (1950), and *I'll Cry Tomorrow* (1956). For each performance she was nominated for an Oscar.

Susan Hayward's footprints are the only ones set in gold dust at Grauman's Chinese Theatre.

Rita Hayworth

Even though Rita Hayworth was once a vocalist with Xavier Cugat's orchestra, Nan Wynn dubbed her singing in the 1944 movie *Cover Girl*. Ann Greer dubbed for her in *Gilda* (1946) and *Pal Joey* (1957).

The atom bomb which was dropped on

Bikini Atoll in 1946 by the B29 "Dave's Dream" was named "Gilda" and had a picture of Rita Hayworth on it.

Rita Hayworth–Susan Hayward

Many people confuse Rita Hayworth with Susan Hayward because of the similarity of their names. To add to the confusion, they were both born in Brooklyn, New York, in 1918.

Rita Hayworth–Grace Kelly

Two Hollywood actresses have married royalty: Rita Hayworth to Prince Aly Khan (1949) and Grace Kelly to Prince Rainier (1956).

Edith Head

Costume designer Edith Head (winner of many, Oscars) taught French and Spanish before her entry into show business. She received a master's degree from Stanford University.

Joey Heatherton

Joey Heatherton's father Ray was the host of the children's TV series *The Merry Mailman*.

Van Heflin

Van Heflin played Phillip Marlowe when the program about the detective first appeared on radio in 1947.

Hellcats of the Navy

In the 1957 Ronald Reagan movie *Hellcats of the Navy* Lloyd M. Bucher played a non-speaking bit role in the submarine film, which was shot aboard the *U.S.S. Besugo*. Bucher would one day become the Captain of the *U.S.S. Pueblo*, the communications ship seized by the North Koreans in 1968.

Hello Dolly!

Hello Dolly! (1969), which starred Barbra Streisand, was directed by dancer Gene Kelly.

Hell's Angels

Four men were killed in various aviation accidents while filming Howard Hughes's 1930 classic *Hell's Angels*.

Brigitte Helm

Brigitte Helm, who played the robotrix in the 1926 German film *Metropolis*, was considered by director James Whale to play the mate of the Monster in *The Bride of Frankenstein* (1935). The part went to Elsa Lanchester.

Margaux Hemingway

Model and actress Margaux Hemingway is the granddaughter of author Ernest Hemingway.

Sonja Henie

Sonja Henie, the Norwegian figure skater, won Gold Medals in the Olympics in 1928, 1932, and 1936. She appeared in several Hollywood productions, but perhaps her greatest achievements were her marriages to three millionaires: Dan Topping, Winthrop Gardner, Jr., and Nils Ostad.

Henry VIII

The role of Henry VIII on the screen has provided the opportunity for three Oscar nominations for Best Actor: Charles Laughton in *The Private Lives of Henry VIII* (1933), Robert Shaw in *A Man for All Seasons* (1966), and Richard Burton in *Anne of the Thousand Days* (1969).

Audrey Hepburn

Audrey Hepburn, born Audry Hepburn-Ruston, is the daughter of a Dutch baroness in Belgium, her country of birth. Her grandfather, Baron Arnoud van Heemstra, was once the governor of Dutch Guiana.

Audrey Hepburn rejected the lead role in both *The Diary of Anne Frank* (1959) and *The Inn of the Sixth Happiness* (1958).

Katharine Hepburn

Both of Katharine Hepburn's parents had master's degrees. Her mother graduated from

Bryn Mawr and Radcliffe, her father from Randolph-Macon and Johns Hopkins. Miss Hepburn was once suspended from Bryn Mawr for smoking a cigarette.

Katherine Hepburn once won a Bronze Medal for figure skating at Madison Square Garden (age: 14). She also won a Connecticut state golf championship (age: 16).

In 1942 Katharine Hepburn was nominated for Best Actress for the movie *Woman of the Year*. In the film she played Tess Harding who is the recipient of the Woman of the Year Award. That same year she became *McCall* magazine's first "Woman of the Year."

Bryn Mawr's M. Carey Thomas Award for outstanding achievement has only been awarded ten times since its creation in 1922. It was awarded in 1977 to 1928 graduate Katharine Hepburn.

Jean Hersholt

Jean Hersholt, in whose honor the Jean Hersholt Humanitarian Award is given at the Academy Awards, was the founder of the Motion Picture Relief Fund.

In 1946 Jean Hersholt was knighted by King Christian X of Denmark.

Irene Hervey

Singer Jack Jones is the son of singer/actor Allan Jones and actress Irene Hervey.

Charlton Heston

During World War II Charlton Heston served as a radio operator in a B25.

Charlton Heston wanted the part of Police Chief Martin Brody in *Jaws* (1975), but he had just finished *Earthquake* (1974) and it was felt that another disaster film would be too much.

Charlton Heston is a recognized artist. His pen and ink drawings have been exhibited in art galleries in the United States and in Europe.

Darryl Hickman

Darryl Hickman, born on July 28, 1931, was named after producer Darryl F. Zanuck by his actress mother Louise La Rue.

Former child actor Darryl Hickman, who is the older brother of actor Dwayne Hickman, is the executive producer of the TV soap opera *Love of Life*. He is married to actress Pamela Lincoln, who appears on the series.

Joe Higgins

Joe Higgins, the sheriff in the Dodge automobile TV commercials, is a major general in the U.S. Air National Guard.

High Sierra

Paul Muni, Edward G. Robinson, and George Raft all turned down the lead role of Roy Earle in the 1941 film *High Sierra*. Humphrey Bogart did not.

Alfred Hitchcock

Although he had been nominated five times for an Academy Award and had been the recipient of the Academy's Irving G. Thalberg Award, Alfred Hitchcock never won an Academy Award for Best Director.

Patricia Hitchcock

Alfred Hitchcock's daughter Patricia doubled for Jane Wyman in the 1950 movie *Stage Fright*.

Eddie Hodges

Eddie Hodges, who played Frank Sinatra's son in the 1959 movie *A Hole in the Head,* won $25,000 on the television quiz show *Name That Tune*.

In 1961 Eddie Hodges had a minor hit record with "I'm Gonna Knock on Your Door."

John Hodiak

Prior to becoming a radio and movie actor John Hodiak was offered a contract with the St. Louis Cardinals farm system. He turned it down in order to become an actor. He was the voice of Li'l Abner on radio.

Dustin Hoffman

Dustin Hoffman's mother named her son after the silent movie star Dustin Farnum.

Hal Holbrook

Hal Holbrook's mother Aileen appeared in *George White's Scandals* (1934) and *Ziegfeld Follies* (1946).

William Holden

William Franklin Beedle was given the name William Holden by a publicist at Paramont Pictures, who named him after a friend who was an associate editor at the *Los Angeles Times*.

William Holden–Robert Ryan

William Holden made his screen debut in the 1939 movie *Golden Boy* as a prize fighter. Robert Ryan made his movie debut in the 1940 film *Golden Gloves* also as a prize fighter. While attending Dartmouth College Ryan became their heavyweight champion, compiling an undefeated record over four years.

Judy Holliday

Judy Holliday, who won a Best Actress Award for her dumb blonde role in *Born Yesterday* (1950), actually had an I.Q. of 172. Her real name was Judith Tuvim. In Hebrew "tuvim" means "holiday."

Sterling Holloway

Sterling Holloway was the first actor drafted into the U.S. Army for World War II. He received a medical discharge after being kicked by a horse.

HOLLYWOODLAND

The familiar sign HOLLYWOOD in the Hollywood Hills used to read HOLLYWOODLAND. Located on Mount Lee, the sign was an advertisement for a land development company. It was from the last letter that actress Peg Entwhistle jumped to her death in 1932.

Hollywood or Bust

Ironically the last movie that Dean Martin (Dino Crocetti) and Jerry Lewis (Joseph Levitch) appeared in together was a 1956 film titled *Hollywood or Bust.*

Georgia Holt

Georgia Holt, the mother of Cher, was beaten out for the lead in the film *The Asphalt Jungle* (1950) by Marilyn Monroe. Wed eight times, Georgia married Cher's father, John Sarkisian, on three different occasions.

Jack Holt

Veteran movie cop Jack Holt was the inspiration for the Fearless Fosdick character created by cartoonist Al Capp.

Tim Holt

During World War II Tim Holt flew twenty-two combat missions in a B29 bomber in the Pacific Theater. He was discharged with the rank of major in 1942. Among his decorations was the Distinguished Flying Cross.

Tim Holt was the only "B" Western hero to smoke in his films. He smoked a pipe.

Hondo

The 1953 movie *Hondo* was originally planned for Glenn Ford, but he had a dispute with director John Farrow, and John Wayne took the part. Although it was filmed in 3-D it was never shown that way.

Darla Hood

Former *Our Gang* star Darla Hood did voice-overs for Chicken of the Sea tuna; she was the voice of the mermaid. She also supplied the voice of a line of talking dolls.

Hopalong Cassidy

The role of Hopalong Cassidy almost went to veteran actor James Gleason. David Niven was also considered.

William Boyd broke a leg in a fall from his white stallion during the filming of *Hopalong Cassidy* in 1935. It was decided to let him limp throughout the movie, supposedly the result of being shot in the leg.

Lee J. Cobb and Robert Mitchum each began their acting careers as bit players in a Hopalong Cassidy picture. Mitchum appeared in a total of eight. So did Chill Wills, the lead singer of the Avalon Boys, who made his film debut in a 1935 Cassidy movie, *Bar-20 Rides Again*.

Bob Hope

Londoners nicknamed German V-2 bombs "Bob Hopes" because people would "bob down and hope for the best."

Bob Hope, while playing a round of golf with Joe Louis, Jimmy McLarin and Fred Astaire, shot a hole-in-one on the 15th hole of the Lakeside golf course. He used a 7-iron.

Contrary to popular belief Bob Hope has been awarded an Oscar on five occasions. He received Special Awards in 1940, 1944, 1952, and 1965. He received the Jean Hersholt Humanitarian Award in 1959.

Bob Hope–Jimmy Durante

Bob Hope once boxed under the name Packy East in Cleveland. Jimmy Durante fought but one time under the name Kid Salerno. He lost.

Miriam Hopkins

Miriam Hopkins played Martha in *These Three* (1936), the first screen version of Lillian Hellman's play. In 1962 she played Aunt Lily in the remake which was titled *The Children's Hour*.

Lena Horne

Lena Horne's grandfather Cyrus Scrottron was the first black railway post-office clerk in the United States.

John Houseman

Actor, producer, and director John Houseman, who played a Harvard Law professor in the 1973 movie *The Paper Chase* and in the 1978-79 TV series, is actually a professor of the performing arts at the University of Southern California.

Leslie Howard

Leslie Howard's daughter, born in October 1924, has the same name as her father. She was named Leslie Ruth Howard. Humphrey Bogart named his daughter Leslie because Howard had aided Bogart when he was a struggling Hollywood contract player.

Leslie Howard was first considered for the part of Dr. Henry Frankenstein in the 1931 movie *Frankenstein.* Colin Clive later got the part.

Leslie Howard took up acting as therapy for shell shock that he suffered during World War I. On December 15, 1939, the night of the Atlanta premiere of *Gone With The Wind,* Howard was the only major star not present because he had returned to England to enlist in the RAF.

Leslie Howard perished when the British Overseas Airways transport plane that he was flying in on June 1, 1943, was shot down by German fighters on a flight from Lisbon to London. It was believed that Winston Churchill would be on the aircraft.

Sydney Howard

Screenwriter Sydney Howard died in a freak tractor accident in the summer of 1939. He was posthumously awarded an Oscar for his screenplay of *Gone With The Wind*, which he never saw in its final form.

Trevor Howard

Trevor Howard has a clause written into all his movie contracts that states he will not work on any day while Britain's International cricket team is playing.

How the West Was Won

One of the Indians who appeared in *How the West Was Won* (1963) was eighty-one-year-old Chief Weasel, a member of the Oglalla tribe and a survivor of the Wounded Knee Massacre.

Rock Hudson

Rock Hudson was a recruit in a class taught by Lieutenant Robert Taylor when they were both in the Navy during World War II.

Howard Hughes

Among his many accomplishments billionaire Howard Hughes claimed to have "discovered" Jean Harlow, Jane Russell, and Marilyn Monroe.

Jeffrey Hunter

Jeffrey Hunter had to shave his armpits for his portrayal of Jesus in the 1961 movie *King of Kings*.

Tab Hunter

Tab Hunter, born Arthur Gelien, was not seen in his first film. His role in the movie *The Lawless* (1950) was edited out of the finished product.

In 1956 Tab Hunter had a number one record with "Young Love."

Ross Hunter

Movie producer Ross Hunter obtained a master's degree in English before his twentieth birthday.

Chet Huntley

Newscaster Chet Huntley played a radio sports announcer in the 1952 movie *The Pride of St. Louis*.

Hush . . . Hush, Sweet Charlotte

Olivia de Havilland replaced the ill Joan Crawford to make the 1965 movie *Hush . . . Hush, Sweet Charlotte*.

John Huston

Director John Huston was a lightweight boxer in his youth. He won twenty-three of twenty-five amateur bouts.

When John Huston decided to film the B. Traven classic *The Treasure of the Sierra Madre* in 1948 he picked a location in Mexico where he had served as a soldier in the Mexican Army in his younger days, San Jose Purua, west of Mexico City. In 1964 he became an Irish citizen.

Walter Huston

As an engineer, prior to becoming an actor, Walter Huston helped to install the plumbing for the small town of Weatherford, Texas, the same town in which actress Mary Martin was born.

In 1938 Walter Huston, father of John Huston, became the first person to record "September Song," introducing it to the public on the Brunswick record label.

Betty Hutton

Betty Hutton was once the female vocalist for the Vincent Lopez band. Her sister Marion once sang with Glenn Miller's orchestra.

Because of her authentic-looking acrobatics in *The Greatest Show on Earth* (1952), the Ringling Bros. and Barnum & Bailey Circus elected Betty Hutton to their Circus Hall of Fame.

I

I Died a Thousand Times

For the 1955 movie *I Died a Thousand Times* Frank Sinatra was to reprise the Roy Earle role that Humphrey Bogart had made famous fourteen years earlier in *High Sierra*. Sinatra wanted 50 percent of the net profits based on his recent Academy Award-winning performance in *From Here to Eternity* (1953). Instead Warner Bros. hired Jack Palance.

I Love Lucy

The original choices to play Fred and Ethel Mertz on TV's *I Love Lucy* were Gale Gordon and Bea Benaderet. However, both had prior commitments and the roles went to William Frawley and Vivian Vance.

When Lucille Ball and Desi Arnaz negotiated the deal for *I Love Lucy* with CBS and Philip Morris they took a $1000 per episode pay cut in return for complete ownership of the series. Desilu later sold the series back to CBS for $4,500,000.

While Philip Morris was the sponsor of *I Love Lucy* the actors were forbidden to use the word "lucky" on the air because of the rival sponsor Lucky Strikes.

Imperial Trio

In 1909 there was a vaudeville team called the Imperial Trio. Its members were known as Leonard, Lawrence, and McKinely. They became better known as Walter Winchell, Jack Wiener, and George Jessel.

In Old Arizona

The successful early talkie *In Old Arizona* (1929) was filmed on location in Utah and California, but no scenes were shot in Arizona.

The Informer–Valley of the Dolls

The 1935 movie *The Informer* premiered onboard the French ocean liner *Normandie*. The 1967 movie *Valley of the Dolls* premiered onboard the Italian cruise ship *MS Princess Italia*.

Rex Ingram

Famous black actor Rex Ingram was born on the riverboat *Robert E. Lee* near Cairo, Illinois.

In the Heat of the Night

The setting for the 1967 movie *In the Heat of the Night* was Sparta, Mississippi. The movie was actually filmed in Sparta, Illinois.

Jill Ireland

Jill Ireland, ex-wife of actor David McCallum and presently the wife of Charles Bronson, appeared in the majority of Bronson's films of the 1970s.

It Happened One Night

Director Frank Capra wanted Robert Montgomery to star in his 1934 film *It Happened One Night* but Montgomery turned down the role. Myrna Loy was to have been his co-star. Loy, Margaret Sullavan, Miriam Hopkins, and Constance Bennett all turned down the female lead. The roles eventually went to Clark Gable and Claudette Colbert, neither of whom wanted to do the picture, but each won the Academy Award for an outstanding performance.

Clark Gable did one scene in *It Happened One Night* shirtless. After the movie was released a measurable drop in sales of men's undershirts was recorded and manufacturers protested.

Burl Ives

Burl Icle Ivanhoe Ives played fullback at Newton High School and Eastern Illinois State Teachers College. He later played for a semi-pro team.

In 1961 Burl Ives made the top-ten chart with a ballad called "A Little Bitty Tear."

Tommy Ivo

Former child actor Tommy Ivo, who appeared in over one hundred movies and was one of the original Mouseketeers on TV's *The Mickey Mouse Club*, has probably driven more miles on a dragstrip than anyone, including Big Daddy Garlits. Today he is a superstar in drag racing.

Ub Iwerks

Ub Iwerks, who was responsible for the special effects used in the 1963 movie *The Birds*, was the actual creator of Mickey Mouse, although his employer (Walt Disney) got the credit.

J

Kate Jackson–Roger Davis

Kate Jackson, formerly one of the stars of *Charlie's Angels*, began her career on television in the soap opera *Dark Shadows* as a ghost named Daphne Harridge. Roger Davis, the ex-husband of another Angel (Jaclyn Smith), was also a regular on *Dark Shadows*.

Jesse James, Jr.

Jesse James, Jr., the son of the notorious outlaw, appeared in a number of films. He was signed to a three-year contract in 1920 at $100,000 a year.

Emil Jannings

The winner of the Best Actor Award at its first presentation was German-born Emil Jannings. He returned to Germany and became an actor for Nazi propaganda movies.

David Janssen

Actor David Janssen's mother, Bernice Dalton, was a former Ziegfeld girl and had been a Miss America runner-up.

While in high school David Janssen won two athletic scholarships and was a two-letter man in track and basketball.

The Jazz Singer

Eddie Cantor turned down *The Jazz Singer* when the 1927 movie was offered to him.

The TV quiz show *Split Second* used the same stage on which Al Jolson appeared in *The Jazz Singer*.

Al Jennings

Silent movie actor Al Jennings was the founder of the Al Jennings Feature Film Company and was technical advisor on Westerns. Previously he had been an outlaw who was personally pardoned by President Theodore Roosevelt.

George Jessel

In his youth George Jessel was a bat boy for the New York Giants baseball club.

George Jessel turned down the film version of *The Jazz Singer* even though he had performed the role on Broadway.

George Jessel–Milton Berle

George Jessel and Milton Berle were born in adjacent buildings on West 118th Street in Harlem.

Ben Johnson

Ben Johnson came to Hollywood in 1940 to wrangle horses for director Howard Hawks in the movie *The Outlaw* at a price of $1.00 a day. Thirty-one years later Johnson won an Oscar for Best Supporting Actor for his work in *The Last Picture Show* (1971).

Rafer Johnson

Black actor Rafer Johnson won the 1960 Olympic decathlon and accumulated 8,392 points.

Rafer Johnson and Rosey Grier were two of Robert F. Kennedy's bodyguards the night he was assassinated at the Ambassador Hotel in Los Angeles (June 5, 1968). Both men wrestled with Sirhan B. Sirhan, taking away his gun.

Van Johnson

Van Johnson turned down the part of Eliot Ness in *The Untouchables*. It was then turned down by Van Heflin before it was accepted by Robert Stack.

Van Johnson—John Payne

Van Johnson and John Payne each appeared as singers in some of their early film work. They were each seriously hurt in car accidents and both had metal plates put in their heads as a result.

Al Jolson

Al Jolson, Babe Ruth, and Bill "Bojangles" Robinson all attended St. Mary's Industrial Home for Boys in Baltimore.

Harry Jolson once sued his brother Al for $25,000 claiming that Al promised to pay him $150 a week not to go into the entertainment business.

Al Jolson wrote the theme song for the 1920 Harding-Coolidge Republican campaign, "Harding, You're the Man for Us."

Al Jolson, who always made an effort to entertain U.S. servicemen, was stricken with pneumonia and malaria after returning from entertaining the troops in October 1943. After a 1950 tour in Korea Jolson was felled by a heart attack and died in San Francisco.

The Jolson Story

Richard Conte, José Ferrer, and Danny Thomas were all considered for the 1946 movie *The Jolson Story*. James Cagney turned the movie down. The Jolson part went to Larry Parks.

Al Jolson appeared in one scene of *The Jolson Story* singing "Swanee." He appeared in blackface and only in long shots. In the 1949 sequel, *Jolson Sings Again*, Larry Parks again played Jolson, but in one scene Parks as Jolson meets the actor Larry Parks.

Buck Jones

Buck Jones, born Charles Gebbart, performed in the circus prior to becoming an actor. He married a circus rider named Odelle Osborne in the center ring during a performance. He was later the father-in-law of Noah Beery, Jr. Buck Jones died as a result of the Boston Cocoanut Grove nightclub fire of November 28, 1942.

Jennifer Jones

Jennifer Jones was May Queen and senior class president of Edgemer Public School in Oklahoma City.

Shirley Jones

Actress Shirley Jones was named by her mother after Shirley Temple. In high school (South Huntingdon High School in Smithton, Pennsylvania) she served as editor of the yearbook. She won the title of Miss Pittsburgh and finished second in the Miss Pennsylvania Beauty Contest.

Stan Jones

Actor and screenwriter Stan Jones is the composer of the classic song "(Ghost) Riders in the Sky."

Victor Jory

Actor Victor Jory was once British Columbia's light heavyweight boxing champion. He was also a National Guard boxing and wrestling champion.

Victor Jory's father delivered the first horses to Skagway, Alaska.

In 1947 Jory narrated the million-selling album *Tubby the Tuna.*

Joyless Street

Actresses Greta Garbo and Marlene Dietrich were both in the 1925 German film *Die Freudlose Gasse* (*Joyless Street*). Miss Dietrich's appearance was unbilled.

Judgment at Nuremberg

In the *Playhouse 90* presentation of the play *Judgment at Nuremberg* the words "gas ovens" were bleeped from the TV dialogue because the program's sponsor was the American Gas Association.

Curt Jurgens

Due to smart real-estate investments Curt Jurgens is the wealthiest actor in West Germany.

K

Duke Kahanamoku

Hawaiian Olympic swimming champion Duke Kahanamoku appeared in the movies *Wake of the Red Witch* (1948) and *Mister Roberts* (1955).

Garson Kanin

Playwright/director Garson Kanin played the part of Rosalie on the radio series *The Goldbergs*.

Boris Karloff

Actor Boris Karloff was rejected by the British Army in World War I because of a heart murmur. Actors Steve Cochran and Jack Carson were rejected by the U.S. Army during World War II because each had a heart murmur.

Boris Karloff helped found the Screen Actors Guild in 1933 and became member #9.

Boris Karloff won $16,000 on the 1950s quiz show *The $64,000 Question*. His subject was Children's Stories.

Boris Karloff–Christopher Lee

Boris Karloff and Christopher Lee have each played the Frankenstein Monster, Dr. Fu Manchu, and the Mummy.

Kurt Kasznar

Actor Kurt Kasznar had two spectacular missions as a U.S. Signal Corps photographer in World War II. He photographed the cities of Hiroshima and Nagasaki following their destruction, and he filmed the Japanese surrender onboard the battleship *U.S.S. Missouri* in Tokyo Bay on September 2, 1945.

Danny Kaye

Danny Kaye has a commercial pilot's license and can pilot a Boeing 747 jumbo jet.

Buster Keaton

Joseph Keaton, the silent film comedian, was given his nickname "Buster" by his godfather, Harry Houdini, when the great magician saw Joseph fall down a flight of backstage stairs as a lad on October 4, 1895.

Helen Keller

Helen Keller, born blind, deaf, and dumb, starred in the 1919 movie *Deliverance*. Patty Duke won an Oscar portraying Keller in the 1962 movie *The Miracle Worker*.

Gene Kelly

As a teenager, entertainer Gene Kelly taught gymnastics at a YMCA camp near Pittsburgh.

Grace Kelly

Grace Kelly's father, John Brendan Kelly, was the National Physical Fitness Director under President Herbert Hoover. He was a Gold Medal winner at the 1920 Olympics in Antwerp in scullracing, singles and doubles.

Grace Kelly's mother, Margaret Majer, was a champion swimmer at Temple University and was once on the cover of the *Saturday Evening Post*. Prior to becoming a successful movie actress, Grace modeled for a number of magazines and appeared in early TV commercials. She was a cover model on *True Story, Cosmopolitan,* and *Redbook*.

The Pulitzer Prize-winning author for drama in 1926 was George Kelly (for *Craig's Wife*), Grace Kelly's uncle.

Grace Kelly appeared in eleven movies. Three of them were directed by Alfred Hitchcock: *Dial M for Murder* (1954), *Rear Window* (1954), and *To Catch a Thief* (1955). Jessie Royce Landis played her mother in both *To Catch a Thief* and *The Swan* (1956).

Paul Kelly

Paul Kelly, who once served time for manslaughter at San Quentin in the 1920s, was cast as the warden in the 1954 movie *Duffy of San Quentin.*

Adam Kennedy

Actor Adam Kennedy, who played Brock Hayden on the TV soap *The Doctors,* is the author of the best-selling novels *The Domino Principle* (also a 1977 movie) and *Love Song.*

Arthur Kennedy–David Wayne

During the Depression years of the 1930s Arthur Kennedy and David Wayne were roommates in New York City before they became well-known actors.

George Kennedy

George Kennedy played unbilled roles on the Phil Silvers program *You'll Never Get Rich,* usually as an Army M.P., since he was actually the Army's technical advisor for the series.

Jacqueline Kennedy

Jacqueline Kennedy won an Emmy while First Lady for a program in which she gave the television audience a tour of the White House.

Kid Galahad

Kid Galahad, the 1937 boxing movie starring Edward G. Robinson, is retitled *The Battling Bellhop* whenever it is shown on television. This came about because of the 1962 remake, *Kid Galahad,* starring Elvis Presley.

Victor Kilian–Charles Wagenheim

Elderly actors Victor Kilian and Charles Wagenheim were both murdered in separate incidents in Hollywood in March 1979. Ironically they had just finished taping an episode of *All in the Family* in which they had both appeared.

The Killers

William Conrad and Burt Lancaster both debuted in the same 1946 motion picture, *The Killers.* A 1964 TV remake of *The Killers* was the last film in which Ronald Reagan appeared.

Miklos Rozsa did the score for *The Killers* (1946). The four notes that were played whenever the killers made an appearance later became the theme for the TV program *Dragnet.*

Kind Hearts and Coronets

Alec Guinness played nine roles in the 1950 English motion picture *Kind Hearts and Coronets.*

Cammie King

Cammie King, who in 1939 played Bonnie Blue Butler in *Gone With The Wind,* never again appeared in a movie; however she did provide the voice of an animated character for a Walt Disney film.

King Kong (1933)

Originally the climax of *King Kong* (1933) was to take place in Yankee Stadium instead of atop the Empire State Building. The original working title for *King Kong* was "The Eighth Wonder."

King Kong producer Merian C. Cooper considered both Jean Harlow and Ginger Rogers for the part of Ann Darrow that ultimately went to Fay Wray.

King Kong was the only film to open simultaneously at the Roxy and a few blocks away at Radio City Music Hall, both in New York City.

In a scene deleted from *King Kong* the great ape dropped a woman from the Empire State Building to her death. The actress was Sandra Shaw (a.k.a. Veronica Balfe) who married Gary Cooper that same year.

The Kiss

The first screen kiss, according to Hollywood legend, was in the 1896 movie *The Kiss*. It was performed by May Irwin and John C. Rice and lasted over thirty seconds. Scenes from *The Kiss* are shown in the 1946 movie *The Spiral Staircase*.

Ted Knight

TV star Ted Knight (Tadewurz Wladizu Konopka) won five Bronze Stars in World War II.

Knights

Among the performers who have been knighted are: John Gielgud, C. Aubrey Smith, Ralph Richardson, Richard Attenborough, John Loder, Cedric Hardwicke, Douglas Fairbanks, Jr., Noel Coward, Alfred Hitchcock, Michael Redgrave, Charles Chaplin, Alec Guinness, and Laurence Olivier (who was the youngest at age forty-one).

Don Knotts

Don Knotts played a catatonic on CBS radio's soap opera *Search for Tomorrow* before becoming a TV series regular.

Elyse Knox

Actress Elyse Knox is the daughter of a former Secretary of the Navy and is the wife of football great Tom Harmon. She is the mother of football star Mark Harmon and her daughter Kristin was married to Rick Nelson.

Ernie Kovacs

Ernie Kovacs smoked an average of twenty cigars each day. He preferred a special brand of Havana cigars which cost him an estimated $13,000 a year.

Stanley Kramer

Producer/director Stanley Kramer and ABC Sports commentator Howard Cosell were fraternity brothers at NYU. Cosell, a major in the U.S. Army at the age of twenty-three, was one of the youngest majors at that time.

Kris Kristofferson

Kris Kristofferson is the son of a retired U.S. Air Force major general. He is a former Golden Gloves boxer and was a Rhodes scholar. He has authored two books and won first prize in a collegiate short-story contest sponsored by the *Atlantic Monthly*. He was a helicopter pilot in the Army and was selected to teach English Literature at West Point. He is a songwriter ("For the Good Times," "Me and Bobby McGee," and "Help Me Make It Through the Night") and recording artist whose records have sold in the millions and is now an established actor. Prior to becoming a recording artist under the Columbia label he was a janitor at their Nashville studio.

Henry Kulky

Character actor and movie heavy Henry "Bomber" Kulky was once the judo champion of South America.

L

Alan Ladd

Actor Alan Ladd was a diving champion in 1932 and also held a 50-yard freestyle record. He once served as a lifeguard at North Hollywood Park. Lee Majors was later a recreational director there.

Alan Ladd (5' 4") stood on a box in many love scenes in order to be taller than his leading lady.

Alan Ladd rejected the part of Jett Rink in *Giant* (1956), and the role went to James Dean. It was Dean's last film role.

Cheryl Ladd

Actress Cheryl Ladd provided the voice of

one of the cats on the TV cartoon series *Josie and the Pussycats.*

In 1978 Cheryl Ladd's recording of "Think It Over" reached number 34 in the Billboard record charts.

The Lady from Shanghai

Orson Welles thought up the title for his 1948 film *The Lady from Shanghai* only because studio executives kept hounding him. In the film there is no character from Shanghai. The yacht *Circe* used in the movie belonged to Errol Flynn who appeared in the movie as an unbilled member of the crew.

Veronica Lake

Veronica Lake once won the title of Miss Florida but had to relinquish it when contest officials discovered that she had lied about her age.

In her first three films Veronica Lake (whose real name was Constance Ockelman) was billed as Constance Keane.

During World War II, the U.S. government asked Veronica Lake to trim her famous peekaboo curls because female munitions workers often caught their long hair in machinery.

Hedy Lamarr

Hedy Lamarr, born Hedwig Eva Maria Kiesler, attended parties in Europe at which

Adolf Hitler and Benito Mussolini were present.

Hedy Lamarr turned down the leading female roles in *Casablanca* (1943), *Gaslight* (1944), and *Laura* (1944).

Hedy Lamarr co-invented a directional system for torpedoes.

Hedy Lamarr–Gene Tierney

Houston oilman W. Howard Lee has been married to both Hedy Lamarr and Gene Tierney.

Dorothy Lamour

Dorothy Lamour, the sarong girl, once sang for the Herbie Day orchestra.

Burt Lancaster–Yul Brynner

Burt Lancaster joined a circus at the age of seventeen and formed an act with Nick Cravat, a character actor who has appeared in several Lancaster films. Yul Brynner also worked for a time as a circus acrobat.

Burt Lancaster–Tony Curtis

Burt Lancaster and Tony Curtis were both born on East 106th Street in New York City. Lancaster was born at home (209 East 106th Street) on November 2, 1913, and Curtis was born at Flower and Fifth Avenue Hospital on

June 3, 1925. The hospital is on East 106th Street.

Michael Landon

Actor Michael Landon once held the national high school record for the javelin throw. His mark of 193 feet, 7 inches, brought him over forty scholarship offers. He chose the University of Southern California.

Allan Lane

The voice of TV's talking horse, Mr. Ed, was that of B-Western star Allan "Rocky" Lane, who had been a college and professional football player before his entry into films. He was a three-letter man at Notre Dame in football, baseball, and basketball.

Jocelyn Lane

Actress Jocelyn Lane, who co-starred with Elvis Presley in the 1965 movie *Tickle Me*, became a princess when she married into British royalty in 1971.

Angela Lansbury

George Lansbury, the grandfather of actress Angela Lansbury, served as leader of the British Labour Party from 1931 to 1935.

In the 1962 movie *The Manchurian Candidate* thirty-seven-year-old Angela Lansbury played the mother of thirty-four-year-old Laurence Harvey.

Rosemary La Planche

Actress Rosemary La Planche has sold over six hundred of her oil paintings, several of them to Richard Nixon.

Jesse L. Lasky–Samuel Goldwyn

Movie moguls Jesse L. Lasky and Samuel Goldwyn were brothers-in-law.

Louise Lasser

Louise Lasser, who played Mary Hartman on television, is the only daughter of tax expert S. Jay Lasser. She is the ex-wife of Woody Allen, and her dog Kefir was once owned by Wally Cox.

Lassie

All dogs that have played Lassie, both in the movies and on TV, have been males.

Lassie has been banned from competing in the annual PATSY Awards because the collies involved have already won a great many of the awards, and it was feared that this animal performer made the competition too tough for other participants. By the way, PATSY has two meanings: Picture Animal Top Star of the Year and Performing Animal Television Star of the Year.

The Last Mile

Clark Gable (in Los Angeles) and Spencer Tracy (in New York) both played Killer Mears in stage productions of *The Last Mile*. Thomas Mitchell also played the part, replacing Tracy. Allen Jenkins later replaced Mitchell.

Charles Laughton

During World War I actor Charles Laughton was gassed while with the Royal Huntingdonshire Regiment. The effects of the gas attack afflicted him for the rest of his life.

Charles Laughton and his actress wife Elsa Lanchester once resided in a house on Dean Street in London's Soho district that had been owned by Karl Marx.

Charles Laughton–Bette Davis

Charles Laughton portrayed King Henry VIII in two movies: *The Private Life of Henry VIII* (1933) and *Young Bess* (1953). Bette Davis portrayed Queen Elizabeth in *The Private Lives of Elizabeth and Essex* (1939) and *The Virgin Queen* (1955).

Charles Laughton–Thomas Mitchell

Charles Laughton passed away on December 16, 1963, one day before actor Thomas Mitchell. They both died at home and had been treated at the same hospital.

"Laura"

"Laura," the title song of the 1944 Otto Preminger movie of the same name starring Gene Tierney as Laura Hunt, was originally titled "Judy" and was written by David Raskin for Judy Garland.

Stan Laurel

Stan Laurel, before teaming with Oliver Hardy to become one of the funniest slapstick teams, was an understudy for comedian Charlie Chaplin.

Stan Laurel, who was married eight times, took Virginia Rogers as his second, third, and seventh wife.

The Law and the Range

The Law and the Range was the first movie made in Hollywood. It was filmed in 1911 by Al Christie.

Peter Lawford

Peter Lawford was the brother-in-law of President John F. Kennedy; he was married to Kennedy's sister Patricia. Lawford later married the daughter of comic Dan Rowan.

Cloris Leachman

Cloris Leachman attended Northwestern University on an Edgar Bergen scholarship.

Bruce Lee

Martial arts expert Bruce Lee won the title of Cha-Cha Champ of Hong Kong in 1958.

In 1963 Bruce Lee was classified as 4-F by his local draft board in Seattle, Washington.

Canada Lee

Black actor Canada Lee was a national lightweight boxing champion and was a contender for the professional welterweight title.

Christopher Lee

Actor Christopher Lee's mother claims to be descended from the Borgias and Charlemagne. His father, Colonel Geoffrey Lee, was a one-time fencing champion of the British Army and also commanded the 60th Kings Royal Rifles. His great-grandfather founded the first operatic company in Australia.

Christopher Lee served with the RAF in World War II and received decorations and medals from Great Britain (six), Czechoslovakia, Yugoslavia, and Poland.

Peggy Lee

Singer Peggy Lee composed the theme music for the movies *Johnny Guitar* (1954) and *The Time Machine* (1960).

Janet Leigh

According to legend Janet Leigh was discovered by actress Norma Shearer at the Sugar

Bowl Ski Lodge in Soda Springs, California, although Miss Leigh was not there. Shearer saw a photo of Janet which her mother kept at the lodge. After sending the photo to Hollywood Miss Leigh was requested by MGM to do a screen test.

Vivien Leigh

Six years before playing the role of Scarlett O'Hara Vivien Leigh was a model for *Vogue* magazine.

Vivien Leigh, the English actress who played Southern belle Scarlett O'Hara in *Gone With The Wind*, was actually born in Darjeeling, India. Miss Leigh took her name from the first name of her first husband, Leigh Holman. Her real maiden name was Vivian Hartley.

Vivien Leigh–Maureen O'Sullivan

Vivien Leigh and Maureen O'Sullivan were classmates and close friends as young ladies when they both attended the Convent of the Sacred Heart at Roehampton, near London. One day Miss O'Sullivan would win the female lead in *A Yank at Oxford* (1939) over Miss Leigh.

Jack Lemmon

Jack Lemmon (born John Uhler Lemmon III), who won an Oscar for his supporting role as Ensign Pulver in the 1955 movie *Mister Roberts*, was actually an ensign during World War II aboard the aircraft carrier *U.S.S. Lake Champlain*.

Jack Lemmon won the Academy Award for Best Actor of 1973 for his role in *Save the Tiger*: yet he was also the recipient of the *Harvard Lampoon*'s Worst Actor of the Year Award for the same performance.

Leo the Lion

The MGM lion, Leo, was first played by Slats. Others have been Jackie, Tanner, and Jackie II.

Alan Jay Lerner

Academy Award-winning lyricist Alan Jay Lerner is the son of the founder of the chain of Lerner clothing stores for women.

Mervyn LeRoy

Future director Mervyn LeRoy experienced the San Francisco earthquake of April 18, 1906, when a lad of six. When he was fifteen he won a Charlie Chaplin contest at the San Francisco World Fair.

Let It Be

Beatles John Lennon and Paul McCartney won an Academy Award for Best Original Song Score for *Let It Be* in 1970.

Letters

Warren Beatty added a "t" to his last name which originally was spelled Beaty. Dionne

Warwicke added an "e" to her last name, War-wick. Lauren Bacall had an "l" added to her mother's maiden name, which had been Bacal. Barbra Streisand took an "a" out of Barbara. Jacqueline Susann added an "n" to her last name, Susan. Carole Lombard added an "e" to Carol. Audry Hepburn-Ruston added an "e" and became Audrey Hepburn. Irene Dunne added an "e" to her last name. Harry Cohn added a "y" to Margarita Cansino's mother's maiden name, Haworth, and she became Rita Hayworth. Vivien Leigh's first name originally was spelled with an "a"—Vivian, but it was stage producer Sydney Carroll who changed the "a" to an "e" so her name would appear more feminine.

Oscar Levant

Pianist, wit, and author Oscar Levant was extremely superstitious, so badly so that anything with the number 13 would make him think instantly of bad luck. He also had a fear of hats, flowers, and hummingbirds, and he stayed out of the sunshine whenever possible.

Jerry Lewis

Since 1951 Jerry Lewis has helped raise over $200 million for his favorite charity, the Muscular Dystrophy Association.

The Life and Times of Judge Roy Bean

Director John Huston made a cameo appearance as Grizzly Adams in the 1972 movie The Life and Times of Judge Roy Bean.

The Life of Riley

Lionel Stander read the role of Chester A. Riley on radio years before William Bendix played the part on television. Prior to Bendix, Jackie Gleason played Riley in the first TV version. Gleason also played the role on radio for a short time. The radio series was originally created with Groucho Marx in mind as Chester.

Lights of New York

Although the 1928 Warner Bros. movie *Lights of New York* holds a niche in film history as one of the first talkies, subtitles were still used throughout the picture.

Elmo Lincoln

The first movie Tarzan was not Elmo Lincoln as is commonly thought. Early on in the first Tarzan movie, *Tarzan of the Apes* (1918), ten-year-old Gordon Griffith is seen as the jungle prince coming before Elmo Lincoln's screen appearance as the adult Tarzan in the same film.

Charles Lindbergh

The hysteria that arose when Charles Lindbergh made his famous flight seemed unreal at times. One film company offered the flier $1,000,000 if he would marry any girl of his choosing while giving them exclusive rights to the filming of the event.

Hal Linden

In 1946 Hal Linden played clarinet with New York's American Symphony Orchestra.

Lines Never Said

Johnny Weissmuller never said "Me Tarzan, you Jane" in the 1932 movie *Tarzan the Ape Man*. He actually said "Tarzan ... Jane" numerous times.

Humphrey Bogart did not say "Play it again, Sam" in the 1943 picture *Casablanca*. What he really said was "You played it for her, you can play it for me. If she can stand it, I can—play it."

Gary Cooper never said "When you call me that, smile!" in the 1929 film *The Virginian*. Cooper said "If you want to call me that, smile!"

A Lion Is in the Streets

A Lion Is in the Streets was a 1953 Warner Bros. film starring James Cagney. His sister Jeanne also appeared in the movie. It was produced by brother Bill and the story editor was Ed Cagney, another brother.

Larry Linville

Larry Linville was born in Ojai, California, the fictitious hometown of both *The Six Million Dollar Man* and *The Bionic Woman*.

Larry Linville, who played Major Frank Burns on the TV series *M*A*S*H*, flunked his physical for the U.S. Air Force.

Larry Linville married Kate Geer, the daughter of the late Will Geer.

Art Linkletter

In 1934 Art Linkletter was an all-conference center on San Diego State's basketball team; he served as the team captain. He also participated in the AAU National Handball Championship and held the 50-yard backstroke title of Southern California.

Little Caesar

Clark Gable made a screen test for the role of Caesar Enrico Bandello in *Little Caesar* (1930). He was rejected by Jack L. Warner who thought him too ugly. Handsome Edward G. Robinson got the part.

Live and Let Die

While filming the 1973 James Bond movie *Live and Let Die*, stuntman Jerry Comeaux had his name immortalized in *The Guinness Book of World Records* when he jumped his racing boat 110 feet over a road.

Harold Lloyd

After 1919, actor Harold Lloyd always wore gloves in his movies because he lost the forefinger and thumb on his right hand in a bomb explosion while posing for publicity pictures in a stunt for the movie *Haunted Spooks.*

Harold Lloyd, who always wore glasses in his movies, had his original glasses insured with Lloyds of London for $25,000, yet they contained no lenses.

Gene Lockhart

Canadian-born actor Gene Lockhart, father of actress June Lockhart, was the Canadian one-mile swimming champion at age eighteen. He also played for the Toronto Argonauts football team.

Gene Lockhart composed the lyrics in 1919 for a song made famous in 1951 by Les Paul and Mary Ford, "The World Is Waiting for the Sunrise." He sang in the opera *Die Fledermaus* in San Francisco.

John Lodge

Actor John Lodge, who appeared in such movies as *Little Women* (1933) and *The Little Colonel* (1935), left the field of acting to become governor of Connecticut in 1950, U.S. Ambassador to Spain in 1955, and in 1968, U.S. Ambassador to Argentina. His actress wife, Francesca Braggiotti, was once named Woman of the Year in Argentina.

The Lodger

In the 1926 movie *The Lodger,* director Alfred Hitchcock found himself without enough extras to complete a scene. In order for the cameras to keep rolling he filled in as a member of the crowd, thus beginning a tradition in his films, a cameo appearance, which has occurred in thirty-five of his movies.

Josh Logan

Director/playwright Josh Logan, while a student at Princeton, was president of the drama society, the Triangle Club.

Lolita

The producers of the 1962 movie *Lolita* wanted Hayley Mills for the lead. It went to Sue Lyon when the Disney people and Hayley's father, John Mills, said no.

Gina Lollobrigida

Gina Lollobrigida won a scholarship to Rome's Academy of Fine Arts where she studied sculpture and painting.

Fidel Castro once gave Gina Lollobrigida a personal interview when the Italian actress began a new career as a photojournalist.

Carole Lombard

Legendary press agent Russell Birdwell once convinced David O. Selznick to declare a certain day Carole Lombard Day, thus making her honorary Mayor of Culver City. Miss Lombard used her authority by declaring the day a real holiday, and sent all the studio employees home. Selznick was quite put out over the incident.

The liberty ship S.S. *Carole Lombard*, launched by Irene Dunne in memory of the work Carole Lombard did in selling U.S. Savings Bonds, was the same ship talk-show host Mike Douglas served on while in the Navy.

The Lonely Man

In the 1953 Jack Palance movie *The Lonely Man* Leo Gordon is credited with playing a role in the film, yet he never appeared.

The Lone Ranger

The Lone Ranger debuted on radio on exactly the same date that Adolf Hitler became Chancellor of Germany—January 30, 1933. It was also the radio program that Julius and Ethel Rosenberg were listening to when arrested in their home by the FBI for their part in giving atomic bomb secrets to the Russians.

Richard Long

Actor Richard Long had a twin sister named Janet.

The Longest Day

The most expensive black and white film ($17,500,000) ever made was the 1962 *The*

Longest Day with an all-star cast. No stock footage of actual battle scenes were used.

The Longest Day was advertised in lights on the Eiffel Tower, the world's largest sign.

Sophia Loren

Sophia Loren's mother, Signora Villani, once won a Greta Garbo look-a-like contest sponsored by MGM.

Maria Villani, the sister of Sophia Loren, married Benito Mussolini's son, Romano. Sophia is the godmother of Mussolini's grandson.

While pregnant with her first child, Sophia Loren wrote a cookbook titled *In the Kitchen with Love*.

Sophia Loren performed her first TV commercials for American television in 1978. She received $1 million to do three thirty-second spots. She gave the money to charity.

Peter Lorre

Peter Lorre was born on June 26, 1904, in a small village in Hungary's Carpathian Mountains, the home of Vlad the Impaler, the legendary basis for Count Dracula.

Lost Horizon (1937 version)

Several men were considered for the role of the High Lama in *Lost Horizon* (1937) before the part went to Sam Jaffe. A.E. Anson and Henry B. Walthall both died before production began. Charles Laughton was also considered.

President Franklin D. Roosevelt was such

a fan of the novel/movie *Lost Horizon* that he called the aircraft carrier *U.S.S. Hornet* Shangri-La as a code for Colonel Jimmy Doolittle's Tokyo raid of April 18, 1942.

The Lost Weekend

In the 1945 movie *The Lost Weekend* Don Birnam (Ray Milland) is handed his hat by a woman as he leaves the bar. Only the woman's arm was shown. It belonged to Loretta Young.

Anita Louise

As a young girl, actress Anita Louise adorned cereal boxes and was well-known as the Post Toasties Girl.

Love Story

Beau Bridges and Robert Redford both turned down the male lead in the 1970 movie *Love Story*. Ryan O'Neal accepted the part.

Loving You

In the 1957 movie *Loving You* Elvis Presley's parents appeared in the film as extras.

Sam Lucas

In the 1914 silent version of *Uncle Tom's Cabin* Sam Lucas became the first black actor to play a lead role in a movie.

Sid Luft

Producer Sid Luft, one-time husband of Judy Garland, was a test pilot for the Douglas Aircraft Company and later served as personal secretary to actress Eleanor Powell.

Bela Lugosi

During World War I Bela Lugosi served as a lieutenant in the Hungarian Army.

Bela Lugosi turned down the part of the Monster in the 1931 classic *Frankenstein* because there were no lines and he thought the make-up was uncomplimentary.

Many times Walt Disney used actual models as cartoon characters for his films. For Tinker Belle (*Peter Pan*, 1953) he used Marilyn Monroe; for Snow White (*Snow White and the Seven Dwarfs*, 1937) he used Marge Champion; and for the model of Tchernobog the Black God in the "Night on Bald Mountain" sequence of *Fantasia* (1940), Bela Lugosi was used as the model.

Bela Lugosi–George Reeves

Bela Lugosi, who died on August 16, 1956, was buried in his Count Dracula cape. George Reeves, who played Superman on TV, died on June 16, 1959, and was buried in the grey double-breasted suit that he wore for years in his Clark Kent role.

Paul Lukas

Actor Paul Lukas was born on a train near Budapest, Hungary on May 26, 1894. He served as a pilot with the Hungarian Air Corps prior to World War I.

Keye Luke

Keye Luke, who is best known for playing Charlie Chan's number-one son, began as a poster painter in Hollywood. He has even painted some of the murals in Grauman's Chinese Theatre.

Keye Luke provided the voice of Charlie Chan in the television cartoon series *The Amazing Chan and the Chan Clan*.

Sidney Lumet

Baruch Lumet, the father of director Sidney Lumet, played bit roles in two of his son's movies: *The Pawnbroker* (1965) and *The Group* (1966).

Sidney Lumet became the son-in-law of singer Lena Horne when he married her daughter Gail.

Ida Lupino

Ida Lupino almost got the part of Alice in 1933's *Alice in Wonderland*, but after her screen test it went to Charlotte Henry.

Peter Lupus

Peter Lupus, who played on the TV series *Mission Impossible*, has held the titles of Mr. Indianapolis, Mr. Indiana, Mr. Hercules, and Mr. International Health.

Lust for Life

During the filming of the 1956 movie *Lust for Life*, starring Kirk Douglas as Vincent Van Gogh, the artist's famous "Yellow House" had to be rebuilt because it had been bombed by American planes during World War II.

Diana Lynn

Actress Diana Lynn was a member of the Los Angeles Junior Symphony Orchestra as a young girl.

Leo Lynn

Bing Crosby's double in his movies was a look-a-like named Leo Lynn. The two first met at Gonzaga College in Seattle, where they became good friends.

Sue Lyon

In 1973, *Lolita* star Sue Lyon married Gary "Cotton" Adamson while he was in Colorado State Penitentiary serving a twenty-to-forty year sentence for murder and armed robbery.

M

M

Director Fritz Lang did the whistling for Peter Lorre in the 1931 classic *M*, Germany's first talking picture.

MGM

"The Lion Roars" was the original motto of MGM pictures before "Ars Gratia Artis" (Art for Art's Sake) was adopted by Howard Dietz.

Jeanette MacDonald

Actress/singer Jeanette MacDonald sang "Ah, Sweet Mystery of Life" at the 1957 funeral of movie mogul Louis B. Mayer.

James MacEachin

James MacEachin, who played a detective on TV's *Tenafly*, formerly worked as both a fireman and a policeman.

Shirley MacLaine

Shirley MacLaine was a delegate to the infamous 1968 Democratic National Convention held in Chicago.

For the 1977 movie *The Turning Point* Shirley MacLaine had an appropriate dance background since she was once a professional ballerina, having taken lessons from the age of two.

Fred MacMurray

In high school, Fred MacMurray won ten letters for various athletic endeavors.

Fred MacMurray was a vocalist for both the George Olsen and Gus Arnheim orchestras. He played saxophone with several bands before becoming an actor. He was a member of the California Collegians in the 1934 play *Roberta* in which Bob Hope appeared leading the band.

Fred MacMurray's face was used as the model for the comic book hero Captain Marvel.

Gordon MacRae

Actor/singer Gordon MacRae was once a vocalist with Horace Heidt's band.

Ted Mack

When he attended Sacred Heart High School in Denver, future *Amateur Hour* host Ted Mack was captain of the football and basketball teams. He was also class president for three years.

The Magic Box

William Friese-Green, sometimes credited as the inventor of the moving picture, who was portrayed in *The Magic Box* (1951) by Robert Donat, was the grandfather of English actor Richard Greene.

The Magic of Lassie

The Magic of Lassie, a 1978 movie starring James Stewart, debuted at New York's Radio City Music Hall, the very same theater at which the original Lassie movie (*Lassie Come Home*) debuted thirty-five years before.

Edgar Magnin

Rabbi Edgar Magnin of the Beverly Wilshire Synagogue converted Marilyn Monroe, Elizabeth Taylor, and Sammy Davis, Jr., to Judaism.

George Maharis

In 1962 actor George Maharis made the record charts with his version of the classic "Teach Me Tonight."

Maisie

The movie series *Maisie*, starring Ann Sothern, was originally planned for Jean Harlow.

The Major and the Minor

In the 1942 movie *The Major and the Minor* Ginger Rogers's real mother, Lela, played her screen mother.

Lee Majors

Lee Majors, star of television's *The Six Million Dollar Man,* was offered a professional football contract with the St. Louis Cardinals during his senior year of college.

Karl Malden

Actor Karl Malden won an athletic scholarship to Arkansas State Teacher's College for being an outstanding basketball star.

Dudley Field Malone

Assistant Secretary of State Dudley Field Malone, who served under President Woodrow Wilson, portrayed Winston Churchill in the 1943 film *Mission to Moscow.*

Henry Mancini

Composer Henry Mancini helped to score (many times uncredited) some of the Francis the Talking Mule movies, Ma and Pa Kettle films, and even *The Creature from the Black Lagoon* (1954).

The Man from U.N.C.L.E.

Ian Fleming, creator of the James Bond character, contributed an idea and worked on pilot scripts that became the TV series *The Man from U.N.C.L.E.*, originally to be called *Solo*.

Jayne Mansfield

Jayne Mansfield once worked as an usherette at Grauman's Chinese Theatre.

"(The Man Who Shot) Liberty Valance"

In 1962 Gene Pitney recorded "(The Man Who Shot) Liberty Valance." The song does not appear as the movie's theme song. However, the movie uses as its theme a score written by Alfred Newman for the 1939 John Ford movie *Young Mr. Lincoln*. Therefore, the theme music of the movie *The Man Who Shot Liberty Valance* comes from *Young Mr. Lincoln*.

Fredric March

Fredric March is the only person to date who has won an Academy Award for Best Actor for playing a monster. In 1931 he made *Dr. Jekyll and Mr. Hyde*.

In the 1946 classic *The Best Years of Our Lives* Fredric March played a bank vice president. Prior to becoming an actor March had been a bank clerk.

Fredric March gave a dramatic reading of Lincoln's Gettysburg Address in 1959 before a joint session of Congress.

Marnie

It was announced that Grace Kelly would come out of retirement to do *Marnie* for Alfred Hitchcock in 1964, but Tippi Hedren eventually played the part, since it was felt that she resembled Grace Kelly.

Herbert Marshall–Ronald Colman

Actors Herbert Marshall and Ronald Colman served in the same regiment in World War I, the 14th London Scots. Both received medical discharges: Marshall lost a leg; Colman received a broken leg.

Penny Marshall

Penny Marshall, who plays Laverne De-Fazio on the TV series *Laverne & Shirley*, is married to Rob Reiner, son of Carl Reiner. Her brother Garry is executive producer of both *Happy Days* and *Laverne & Shirley*.

Peter Marshall

Peter Marshall's son, Pete La Cock, plays professional baseball with the Kansas City Royals. Marshall's sister is Joanne Dru, who was once married to actor John Ireland.

Dean Martin

Dean Martin fought as a welterweight in his youth and won twenty-four of his thirty bouts.

Strother Martin

Character actor Strother Martin was inducted into the Swimming Hall of Fame.

Tony Martin

Singer, actor Tony Martin played saxophone in the Navy Blue Blowers Band in the 1936 Fred Astaire-Ginger Rogers film *Follow the Fleet*.

Marty

Harold Hecht and Burt Lancaster's company produced the 1955 movie *Marty*, which won Best Picture, Best Actor, Best Director, and Best Writing Awards.

Lee Marvin

Lee Marvin is a descendant of the first chief justice of the state of Connecticut, Matthew Marvin.

Lee Marvin receives a 100 percent disability pension from the government due to a wound he received while fighting in the Pacific during World War II. He suffered a severed sciatic nerve.

Deep-sea fisherman Lee Marvin has landed seven marlins weighing over 1000 pounds each.

In 1970 Lee Marvin received a Gold Record for his million-selling 45 rpm "Wand'rin Star" (from the 1969 movie *Paint Your Wagon*).

Lee Marvin was involved in a landmark California court decision in 1979 involving Michelle Triola, the woman he lived with from 1964 to 1970. She was awarded $104,000.

Marx Brothers

Four of the Marx brothers: Groucho, Chico, Harpo, and Gummo were given their names by monologuist Art Fisher from the comic strip *Mager's Monks*.

Chico Marx

In 1942 and 1943 Chico Marx had his own dance band, which was organized by Ben Pollack. Mel Torme sang with the Marx's group.

Groucho Marx

Comedian Groucho Marx, who never broke 90 in a golf game, once shot a hole in one at Boston's Brae Burn Country Club.

Groucho Marx was set to play Chester A. Riley on the radio series, but no sponsor could be found. Ultimately Jackie Gleason, William Bendix, and Lionel Stander each played the role on radio. Gleason and Bendix also played the part on television.

Harpo Marx

Fifty-five-thousand dollars was offered to Harpo Marx if he would speak but a single word —"Murder!" for the 1946 Marx brothers film *A Night in Casablanca*. Had he accepted, publicity would have billed the movie "Harpo Speaks."

Zeppo Marx

While Groucho, Chico, and Harpo were cutting up the screen with their antics, brother Zeppo was running a talent agency that represented such performers as Barbara Stanwyck, Robert Taylor, Carole Lombard, and Clark Gable.

Zeppo Marx was granted a U.S. patent for a wristwatch that can also check a person's heartbeat.

Jackie Mason

Comic Jackie Mason once sold Perry Como a pair of pajamas while working as a sales clerk at Saks Fifth Avenue. Years later Mason would appear on Como's TV show as a guest.

Raymond Massey

Actor Raymond Massey's ancestors arrived in America in 1629 and settled in Salem, Massachusetts.

Joyce Mathews

Joyce Mathews married Milton Berle in 1941,
Joyce Mathews divorced Milton Berle in 1947,

Joyce Mathews married Milton Berle in
1949,
Joyce Mathews divorced Milton Berle in
1950,
Joyce Mathews married Billy Rose in 1956,
Joyce Mathews divorced Billy Rose in 1959,
Joyce Mathews married Billy Rose in 1961,
Joyce Mathews divorced Billy Rose in 1963.

Walter Matthau

Actor Walter Matthau's father Melas Ma-
tuschanskayasky, had been a Catholic priest
in Czarist Russia prior to marrying Walter's
mother.

Victor Mature

Actor Victor Mature once won the Pro-Am
Golf Championship held at the Long Beach
Municipal Golf Course in California.

Bill Mauldin

Cartoonist Bill Mauldin played a soldier in
the 1951 movie *The Red Badge of Courage*.

Marilyn Maxwell

Marilyn Maxwell's real first name was Marvel. She once sang with the bands of both Ted
Weems and Buddy Rogers.

Louis B. Mayer

Producer Louis B. Mayer was the one-time
owner of Busher, the greatest money-winning
fillie in turf history.

Ken Maynard

Before becoming a hero in Western movies Ken Maynard was a rider for the Ringling Bros. and Barnum & Bailey Circus.

Kermit Maynard

Kermit Maynard, older brother of Ken, appeared in numerous silent Westerns billed as Tex Maynard. He was the 1931 and 1933 World Champion Rodeo Trick Rider and Fancy Rider.

May 27

Horror-film masters Vincent Price, Peter Cushing, and Christopher Lee share the same birthday, May 27.

Mike Mazurki

Screen heavy Mike Mazurki was a wrestler before entering show business. He has also worked as a referee for wrestling matches.

David McCallum

The father of David McCallum (who played agent Illya Kuryakin on the TV series *The Man from U.N.C.L.E.*) was a first violinist with the London Philharmonic Orchestra and with Mantovani's Orchestra.

Mercedes McCambridge

Actress Mercedes McCambridge provided the unbilled voice of the demon in the 1973 movie *The Exorcist*.

Charlie McCarthy

Ventriloquist Edgar Bergen left his dummy, Charlie McCarthy, $10,000 in his will, via the Actor's Fund, to see that Charlie is kept in good repair. The dummy's original name was Charlie Mack, named for the man who carved him.

Kevin McCarthy

Actor Kevin McCarthy is the brother of author Mary McCarthy (*The Group*).

Tim McCoy

Cowboy star Tim McCoy made a cameo appearance in the 1956 spectacular *Around the World in Eighty Days* as a cavalry colonel. In actuality he rose to the rank of colonel during World War I. He is one of the country's leading authorities on the American Indian. During World War II he was awarded the Bronze Star.

Joel McCrea

Actor Joel McCrea was once a paperboy for silent star William S. Hart.

Joel McCrea was a stunt-double for Greta Garbo in a horse-riding sequence in Garbo's first American film, *The Torrent* (1926).

Joel McCrea was originally announced as the male lead in *King Kong* (1933). The part went to Bruce Cabot.

Lew Ayres was not the first actor to play

Dr. Kildare in the movies. Joel McCrea played the role in 1937's *Internes Can't Take Money*.

Hattie McDaniel

In the 1937 movie *Saratoga* Hattie McDaniel was accidentally credited as Hattie McDaniels.

Hattie McDaniel, the first black to win an Oscar (for Best Supporting Actress for *Gone With The Wind*), was also the first black female to sing on radio.

Hattie McDaniel–Louise Beavers

Hattie McDaniel and Louise Beavers, who both played *Beulah* on television, died on the same day ten years apart, October 26, 1952, and October 26, 1962, respectively.

Roddy McDowall

Roddy McDowall's sister Virginia was once Montgomery Clift's private secretary.

Gardner McKay

Gardner McKay, while a passenger on the liner *Ile de France*, shot many rescue pictures of the *Andrea Doria* survivors after the ship collided with the *Stockholm* on July 25, 1956.

Victor McLaglen

Actor Victor McLaglen was once a member of the London Guards, joining when he was fourteen years old. He later fought in the Boer War. He also served as provost marshal of Baghdad, Iraq.

Victor McLaglen was once a heavyweight boxer prior to becoming an actor. He even fought heavyweight champion Jack Johnson in a non-title bout on March 10, 1909, in Vancouver, British Columbia. Six rounds, no decision.

Ed McMahon

Ed McMahon, Johnny Carson's late-night straight man, played a clown on the TV show *Big Top* in the early 1950s.

Barbara McNair

Arthur Godfrey's *Talent Scouts* winner Barbara McNair became the first black to be included in the ten most-beautiful list of the International Cosmetologists Society.

Butterfly McQueen

Thelma McQueen obtained her nickname "Butterfly" when she danced in the Butterfly Ballet in the play *A Midsummer Night's Dream* in Harlem.

Steve McQueen

Steve McQueen once spent forty-one days in the brig for going AWOL while a member of the U.S. Marines.

To dispel a myth, Steve McQueen did not

do all of the motorcycle driving in *The Great Escape* (1963), nor of the Mustang in the 1968 movie *Bullitt*. Jeff Smith, a British biker, did the jump in *The Great Escape*, and in *Bullitt* Bud Ekins and Carey Loftin did part of the driving.

Steve McQueen and co-driver Peter Revson finished second in the 1970 Sebring Race behind Mario Andretti.

Audrey Meadows

At age sixteen Audrey Meadows sang as coloratura soprano in Carnegie Hall. She can hit E above high C. She later designed the interior of the Continental Airlines DC-10's first-class section.

Audrey Meadows–Jayne Meadows

Sisters Audrey and Jayne Meadows were born in Wu Chang, China. Their parents were missionaries.

Donald Meek

Actor Donald Meek lost his hair as a young man of eighteen because he contracted a tropical fever while with the American forces in the Spanish-American War.

Meet John Doe

Frank Capra filmed five different endings to the 1941 Gary Cooper movie *Meet John Doe*.

Adolphe Menjou

Famous character actor Adolphe Menjou served as a captain with the U.S. Ambulance Corps in World War I.

Dina Merrill

Actress Dina Merrill, born Nedinia Hutton, is the heiress to the Post cereal fortune and is the daughter of the late multi-millionaire stockbroker E. F. Hutton. She is married to actor Cliff Robertson.

Frank Merrill

Tarzan Frank Merrill was the 1916-1918 National Gymnastics Champion, winning over fifty meets.

Mildred Pierce

For the 1945 movie *Mildred Pierce* director Michael Curtiz wanted Barbara Stanwyck. Studio chief Jack Warner wanted Ann Sheridan. Producer Jerry Wald was adamant in his choice of Joan Crawford who won the Best Actress Oscar for the role.

Vera Miles

Vera Miles (Miss Kansas of 1948) had to change her name from Vera Ralston since there was already an actress by that name.

Ray Milland

Ray Milland was once a jockey in the Grand National Steeplechase. He also served as a member of the King's Household Cavalry at Buckingham Palace as a young man.

Ann Miller

Ann Miller was the first tap dancer ever to appear on TV.

Million Dollar Legs

The title *Million Dollar Legs* of that 1939 movie did not refer to Betty Grable, one of its stars. It referred to the valuable football team at fictional Midland College.

Hayley Mills

Actress Hayley Mills had a national hit record in 1961 with "Let's Get Together."

John Mills

John Mills won an Academy Award in 1971 for his role as a deaf mute in *Ryan's Daughter* (1970). When he accepted his Oscar he did not say a word.

Juliet Mills

Juliet Mills, daughter of John and sister of Hayley, made her motion picture debut as the eleven-week-old baby of Shorty Burke (John Mills) in the 1942 movie *In Which We Serve*.

Sal Mineo

In April 1957 actor Sal Mineo had a top-forty hit with the song "Start Movin'."

Liza Minnelli

Whenever Liza Minnelli is asked to sing "Over the Rainbow" her usual reply is "It's already been sung."

Liza Minnelli won a Tony in 1965 (*Flora, the Red Menace*), an Emmy in 1972 (*Liza with a Z!*), and an Oscar in 1973 (*Cabaret*).

In 1978 Liza Minnelli purchased a portrait of herself painted by Andy Warhol for $25,000.

Liza Minnelli, daughter of Judy Garland, who played Dorothy in *The Wizard of Oz*, has been married to Jack Haley, Jr., the son of Jack Haley, who played the Tin Woodsman in that 1939 movie. They were divorced in 1979.

Carmen Miranda

Singer/dancer Carmen Miranda's career was ruined when it was found that she danced without wearing any underwear in films.

Margaret Mitchell

Margaret Mitchell's father had been president of the Atlanta Historical Society. This provided Miss Mitchell with much information in writing her novel *Gone With The Wind*.

Thomas Mitchell

Actor Thomas Mitchell was the uncle of James Mitchell, former U.S. Secretary of Labor under President Dwight D. Eisenhower.

Robert Mitchum

Robert Mitchum has served three different jail sentences.

He fought in twenty-seven professional heavyweight fights.

In 1939 Robert Mitchum composed an oratorio that was directed by Orson Welles and was performed at the Hollywood Bowl.

Robert Mitchum made his television debut in April 1956, on the Dorsey Brothers' *Stage Show;* Mitchum sang on the program. It was on this same program that Elvis Presley made his television debut three months earlier.

Tom Mix

Contrary to popular opinion and early studio publicity, actor Tom Mix never left the U.S. mainland during the Spanish-American War. He never fought in Cuba or the Philippines, did not fight in the Boer War, and was not a deputy U.S. marshal. In fact, Mix went AWOL and was eventually listed as a deserter.

Tom Mix's daughter Ruth appeared in several Western films against the will of her father.

Tom Mix never played himself on radio. Those who did were Artells Dickson, Russell Thorson, Jack Holden, and Curley Bradley.

On October 12, 1940, Western star Tom Mix was killed in his Cord Roadster near Florence, Arizona. Exactly two years later to the day, October 12, 1942, his famous horse Tony passed away.

Tom Mix and other Western stars Buck Jones, Tim McCoy, and Sunset Carson are all members of the Circus Hall of Fame, located in Baraboo, Wisconsin.

Tom Mix–Yakima Canutt–Slim Pickens

Tom Mix, Yakima Canutt, and Slim Pickens were all rodeo stars at one time. Slim Pickens fought over 3000 bulls and at one time was the highest paid rodeo clown.

Tom Mix–Bela Lugosi

Tom Mix was born in Mix Run, Pennsylvania. Bela Lugosi was born in Lugosi, Hungary.

Mogambo

Mogambo was filmed in 1953 and starred Clark Gable and Ava Gardner. It was a remake of the 1932 movie *Red Dust* which starred Clark Gable and Jean Harlow.

The Monkees

NBC received more letters protesting the cancellation of *The Monkees* than for the cancellation of any series, including *Star Trek*.

Monkey Business

Sam "Frenchie" Marx, father of the Marx Brothers, appeared as an extra in their 1931 film *Monkey Business*.

Marilyn Monroe

Marilyn Monroe claimed to be a descendant of President James Monroe through her grandmother on her mother's side. Her grandmother was named Della Hogan Monroe Grainger.

Marilyn Monroe's real name was Norma Jean Mortenson. Her mother named her in honor of two popular actresses: Norma Talmadge and Jean Harlow.

Marilyn Monroe was the first centerfold for Hugh Hefner's magazine *Playboy* in December 1953. This was the only time that the centerfold girl was referred to as "Sweetheart of the Month."

Marilyn Monroe–Kim Kovak

Kim Novak, sometimes considered another Marilyn Monroe, was born Marilyn Novak.

George Montgomery

George Montgomery was a heavyweight boxing champion in the Pacific Northwest during his freshman year in college. He began his career in films as a stand-in for John Wayne.

George Montgomery has had several of his

sculptures on exhibition. Some works have been valued at over $5,000.

Robert Montgomery

Actor Robert Montgomery, who commanded PT boats near the Panama Canal in World War II, played a PT boat commander in the 1945 film *They Were Expendable*. In 1947 he was made a knight in the French Legion of Honor.

Months

May Robson was born in April; Lois January was born in October; Fredric March was born in August; June Allyson was born in October; June Knight was born in January; June Havoc was born in November (but her daughter April *was* born in April); June Haver was actually born in June.

Archie Moore

Former light-heavyweight boxing champ Archie Moore played a butler in *The Carpetbaggers* (1964), Alan Ladd's last American film.

Clayton Moore

Clayton Moore, who spent several years as TV's *The Lone Ranger*, is a former trapeze artist and was once a model for the John Robert Powers Agency.

Cleo Moore

Actress Cleo Moore was the daughter-in-law of former Louisiana Governor Huey P. Long.

Colleen Moore

Silent screen star Colleen Moore had one blue eye and one brown eye.

Colleen Moore authored several books after retiring as an actress. One of her works is *How Women Can Make Money in the Stock Market*.

Mary Tyler Moore

Mary Tyler Moore's first show business work came as a pixie in Happy Hotpoint commercials on the TV series *Ozzie and Harriet*. A few years later she played an answering service girl on the *Richard Diamond* TV series that starred David Janssen. Mary played a girl named Sam and could only be identified by her voice and legs. She left the series after thirteen episodes and was replaced by Roxanne Brooks.

Terry Moore

Actress Terry Moore learned to fly an airplane from the man she claims to have once been married to, Howard Hughes. Today Terry Moore is the president of North Star Aircraft Corporation.

Agnes Moorehead

Agnes Moorehead attended Muskingum College in Ohio which was founded by her uncle. The learning institution conferred several honors on her.

Rita Moreno–Liza Minnelli

Rita Moreno and Liza Minnelli are the only entertainers to have won an Oscar, an Emmy, a Tony, and a Grammy Award.

Dennis Morgan

Dennis Morgan played semi-pro baseball in the Northern Wisconsin league prior to becoming an actor.

Frank Morgan

Frank Morgan played five roles in *The Wizard of Oz*: Professor Marvel, the Wizard, the Gateman, the driver of the horse of a different color, the Wizard's guard.

In 1947 Frank Morgan won the Annual Honolulu Sailboat race in his boat *Dolphin*.

Harry Morgan

Character actor Harry Morgan's first name is Henry. He used Harry so that he would not be confused with television panelist Henry Morgan. Harry Morgan was born Henry Bratsburger.

Robert Morley

Actor Robert Morley married Joan Buckmaster, daughter of actress Gladys Cooper.

Chester Morris

Adrian Morris, who played a carpetbagger in *Gone With The Wind,* is the brother of actor Chester Morris.

Glenn Morris

Tarzan Glenn Morris once played pro-football with the Detroit Lions.

Wayne Morris

Wayne Morris shot down seven Japanese aircraft and sank two destroyers during World War II. He was awarded four Distinguished Flying Crosses. He enlisted as an ensign and was discharged as a lt. commander. On September 14, 1959, Morris collapsed and died of a heart attack while onboard the aircraft carrier *U.S.S. Bonhomme Richard* off the California coast. The vessel was commanded by his wife's uncle, Captain David MacCampbell.

Patricia Morrow

Patricia Morrow made her movie debut playing the two-week-old baby of Theo Scofield West (Lana Turner) in the 1944 movie *Marriage Is a Private Affair.*

Zero Mostel

Zero Mostel, born Samuel Joel Mostel in 1915, received his nickname "Zero" in elementary school because he was such a poor student.

Movie props

Some of the props that are used in movies are very interesting. In the 1929 Marx Brothers' movie *Cocoanuts* Harpo did not really eat a telephone and drink a bottle of ink. He really had a chocolate telephone and drank Coca-Cola out of an inkwell. In *Singin' in the Rain* (1952) milk was added to the rain water so that the raindrops could be filmed. Janet Leigh's blood in the shower scene of *Psycho* (1960) was really chocolate sauce. (Actually neither Janet Leigh nor Tony Perkins played in the final recorded sequence—two stunt actors were used.) In the 1925 silent movie *The Gold Rush,* the shoe that Charlie Chaplin ate was made out of licorice at a cost of $200.

Movie roles

A few times actors have played the same role in several movies. James Mason portrayed General Erwin Rommel in *The Desert Fox* (1951) and *The Desert Rats* (1953). Charlton Heston portrayed Andrew Jackson in *The President's Lady* (1953) and again in *The Buccaneer* (1958). Raymond Massey portrayed John Brown in *Santa Fe Trail* (1940) and *Seven Angry Men* (1955). Edward Arnold portrayed Diamond Jim Brady in *Diamond Jim* (1935) and in *Lillian Russell* (1940). Joseph Crehan portrayed Ulysses S. Grant in four movies (*see* Joseph Crehan).

Mister Roberts

Henry Fonda had not made a film in several years when *Mister Roberts* was to be brought to the screen in 1955. Producer Leland Hayward talked about bringing in a sure-fire box office name instead of Fonda. Both Marlon Brando and William Holden were suggested. Director John Ford refused to go ahead with the project without Fonda. Ford was later replaced by Mervyn LeRoy.

Mrs. Miniver

The title role of the 1942 movie *Mrs. Miniver* almost went to Norma Shearer, Irving Thalberg's widow. She turned it down because she did not want to play the mother of an adult son. Greer Garson then received the part and later married actor Richard Ney who played her son in the movie.

President Franklin D. Roosevelt was so impressed with the closing speech made in *Mrs. Miniver* that he had it printed on leaflets and dropped over Nazi-occupied Europe.

Paul Muni

Ironically, Paul Muni's last movie was titled *The Last Angry Man* (1959) for which he was nominated for Best Actor.

George Murphy

George Murphy's father was a track coach for the 1912 Olympic team that Jim Thorpe ran for in Stockholm, Sweden.

George Murphy was a singer for both the Emil Coleman and George Olsen bands. After forsaking his acting career he became a U.S. Senator from California.

George Murphy–Eva Marie Saint

George Murphy and Eva Marie Saint were both born on the Fourth of July in 1904 and 1924, respectively. Miss Saint worked for a time as a tour guide at NBC in New York.

Mutes

Jane Wyman (*Johnny Belinda,* 1948), Patty Duke (*The Miracle Worker,* 1962) and John Mills (*Ryan's Daughter,* 1970) all won Oscars for playing mutes.

Mutiny on the Bounty (1935 version)

Mutiny on the Bounty was first planned with Wallace Beery and Robert Montgomery in the roles later played by Charles Laughton and Franchot Tone.

David Niven played an unbilled extra in the 1935 classic *Mutiny on the Bounty,* as did James Cagney. They were both on the set for only one day's shooting. It was Niven's movie debut.

The only time that three actors from the

same film have been nominated for Best Actor was in 1935 for *Mutiny on the Bounty*. Clark Gable, Charles Laughton, and Franchot Tone were all nominated. And the winner is ... Victor McLaglen for *The Informer*.

My Darling Clementine

John Ford, who directed *My Darling Clementine*, the 1946 movie about the life of Wyatt Earp, actually knew the famous Marshal.

My Fair Lady

George Sanders, Noel Coward, and Michael Redgrave all turned down the stage role of Professor Higgins in *My Fair Lady*.

N

Jim Nabors

Actor/singer Jim Nabors once worked as a typist at the United Nations.

J. Carrol Naish

John Naish, the great-grandfather of actor J. Carroll Naish, was the Lord Chancellor of Ireland.

J. Carroll Naish deserted the U.S. Navy to join the U.S. Army during World War I.

J. Carroll Naish (first name Joseph) was born in New York and was Irish by ancestry, yet he played Italians, Indians, Chinese, Japanese, Englishmen, and blacks on the screen.

National Velvet

MGM once considered making *National Velvet* with Spencer Tracy and Shirley Temple.

The horse named Pi (short for Pibald) that Elizabeth Taylor rode in the 1944 movie *National Velvet* was actually named King Charles and was a grandson of the famous Man o' War. On her fourteenth birthday the studio (MGM) presented Miss Taylor with the horse as a present.

Naughty Marietta

The song "Ah, Sweet Mystery of Life" was the theme song of Forest Lawn Cemetery before it was used in the 1935 movie *Naughty Marietta*.

Tom Neal

Muscular actor Tom Neal served a seven-year sentence in a California state prison for the involuntary manslaughter of his third wife.

Noel Neill

One of television's Lois Lanes on *The Adventures of Superman,* actress Noel Neill, actually worked as a reporter for *Women's Wear Daily*.

Ozzie Nelson

Ozzie Nelson, born Oswald George Nelson, was graduated from Rutgers University with a law degree. At the age of thirteen he was the youngest Eagle Scout in the United States.

Never a Dull Moment

Never a Dull Moment (1950) won the *Harvard Lampoon*'s Dullest Movie Award.

Paul Newman

Prior to Paul Newman's appearance in his first movie, *The Silver Chalice* (1954), he had appeared in the TV series *The Aldrich Family*.

Paul Newman was the only actor to be included on Richard Nixon's original list of twenty enemies. Newman was on the list because of his involvement in liberal causes in 1972.

Paul Newman, a professional automobile driver, won the President's Cup by finishing first at the Road Atlanta in Atlanta, Georgia, in November 1976. Newman was part of a team that finished second at Le Mans on June 10, 1979. The other drivers were Dick Barbour of San Diego and Rolf Stommelen of Germany. The car was a Porsche 935 twin turbo coupe.

Paul Newman–James Dean

The role played by Paul Newman in *The Silver Chalice* was originally turned down by James Dean. Newman was beat out by Dean for *East of Eden* (1955). Dean was set to play the lead in *Somebody Up There Likes Me*

(1956), but was killed in a car accident on September 30, 1955. He was replaced by Paul Newman.

Julie Newmar

Actress Julie Newmar has been issued patents for bras, garter belts, and pantyhose.

New Trier High School

Ralph Bellamy, Hugh O'Brian, Cloris Leachman, Rock Hudson, Ann-Margret, and Charlton Heston all attended the same high school in Winnetka, Illinois—New Trier High School. Heston went on to Northwestern University's School of Speech and had Patricia Neal and Ralph Meeker as classmates.

The Night of the Hunter

Actor Charles Laughton directed only one movie, *The Night of the Hunter* (1955). It starred Robert Mitchum.

Nine movies

Katharine Hepburn and Spencer Tracy appeared together in nine movies. Greer Garson was married to Walter Pidgeon in nine movies.

1939

The year 1939 is considered by many movie buffs to have been the most productive single year for great movies. For example: *Goodbye Mr. Chips, Wuthering Heights, Ninotchka, Of Mice and Men, Mr. Smith Goes to Washington, Dark Victory, Beau Geste, Gunga Din, Young Mr. Lincoln, Destry Rides Again, Stagecoach, The Hunchback of Notre Dame, Union Pacific, Drums Along the Mohawk, Love Affair, The Wizard of Oz, Babes in Arms,* and the immortal *Gone With the Wind.* The Academy Awards for 1939 were presented on February 29, 1940, and no one was surprised when it was announced that *Gone With The Wind* had won the Best Picture Award.

David Niven

Although he was listed as Anglo-Saxon Type No. 2008 by central casting upon his arrival in Hollywood, David Niven's first major movie role was that of a Mexican.

During World War II it was supposedly David Niven's idea to have Clifton James, a British soldier, act as Field Marshal Bernard L. Montgomery's double. This feat was planned to confuse the Germans of Montgomery's actual whereabouts. Niven graduated from Sandhurst, England's equivalent to West Point.

David Niven was Ian Fleming's first choice to play James Bond in the movies.

Kathy Nolan

In 1975 actress Kathy Nolan became the first woman to be elected President of the Screen Actors Guild.

No Man of Her Own

One of Hollywood's best-loved couples, Carole Lombard and Clark Gable, appeared together in only one movie, *No Man of Her Own* (1932).

Tommy Noonan

The late Tommy Noonan, formerly a comedy partner of Peter Marshall, was the brother of actor John Ireland.

Mabel Normand

Actress Mabel Normand was once a professional model. She posed for such famous artists as Charles Dana and James Montgomery Flagg.

Jay North

When television's *Dennis the Menace*, Jay North, joined the U.S. Navy in January 1977, he was administered the recruit's oath by Reserve Navy Captain Jackie Cooper.

Norwood

Norwood was a 1970 movie starring Glen Campbell and Joe Namath. It was directed by Jack Haley, Jr., and in the film Jack Haley, Sr. played the father of Joe Namath.

Nose

The oversized nose that José Ferrer sported in the 1950 movie *Cyrano de Bergerac* reportedly cost over $5,000, which covered illustrations, material, and labor.

Ramon Novarro

Actor Ramon Novarro was the second cousin of actress Dolores Del Rio.

Now, Voyageur

Ten years before Paul Henreid lit two cigarettes for himself and Bette Davis in *Now, Voyageur* (1942) George Brent performed the same task for Miss Davis in *The Rich Are Always with Us.*

Number Thirteen

The only movie that director Alfred Hitchcock has ever failed to complete was begun in 1922. It was titled *Number Thirteen.* Funds ran out.

O

Philip Ober

Character actor Philip Ober (once married to Vivian Vance) has served as an acting U.S. Representative for the American Consul in Guadalajara.

Objective, Burma!

The movie *Objective, Burma!* (1945) was banned in England for several years because it placed too much emphasis on U.S. involvement in the Burma campaign.

Hugh O'Brian

At the age of eighteen actor Hugh O'Brian became one of the youngest drill instructors in the history of the Marine Corps. His father was a Marine captain.

George O'Brien

Actor George O'Brien's father was Police Chief of San Francisco.

George O'Brien won the light-weight boxing title of the Pacific Fleet while he was in the U.S. Navy. During World War II he took part as an officer in fifteen invasions.

Pat O'Brien

Actor Pat O'Brien once worked as a young boy lining a football field for a game in which Notre Dame great Knute Rockne played.

Arthur O'Connell

Character actor Arthur O'Connell was captain of his college debate team and during World War II served as an instructor at West Point.

Carroll O'Connor

Both of Carroll O'Connor's brothers have become physicians.

Donald O'Connor

Donald O'Connor has written symphonic compositions and has conducted the Los Angeles Philharmonic Orchestra.

Jack O'Halloran

Movie heavy Jack O'Halloran is the former heavyweight boxing champion of California.

John O'Hara

Novelist John O'Hara appeared in the 1936 movie *The General Died at Dawn* in a bit part as a reporter on a train.

Maureen O'Hara

In March 1968 Maureen O'Hara married Charles Blain for the third time. He is a Pan American pilot who in 1951 became the first man to solo over the North Pole in a single-engined aircraft.

Dennis O'Keefe

Actor Dennis O'Keefe wrote several screenplays under the nom de plume Jonathan Ricks.

Warner Oland

Warner Oland, who played Charlie Chan from 1931 to 1937, once taught at Harvard University.

Laurence Olivier

Laurence Olivier has long enjoyed a reputation as a fine Shakespearean actor. His acting debut came at the age of fifteen when he appeared as Katharine in a production of *The Taming of the Shrew.*

Laurence Olivier was knighted on July 8, 1947. His former wife, Vivien Leigh, died on July 8, 1967, exactly twenty years later.

Ryan O'Neal

Ryan O'Neal's father, Charles O'Neal, was a Hollywood writer.

In 1970 Ryan O'Neal won the Los Angeles Silver Annual Handball Tournament. He once boxed in the West Coast Golden Gloves.

Tatum O'Neal–George Burns

Tatum O'Neal is the youngest person (at age ten) to win an Oscar. She received an Academy Award as Best Supporting Actress of 1973 for *Paper Moon.* The oldest person to be awarded an Oscar is George Burns who won as Best Supporting Actor of 1975 for *The Sunshine Boys* at the age of eighty. Jack Benny was scheduled to play the George Burns role but due to illness could not.

One Flew Over the Cuckoo's Nest

The part of Nurse Ratched in *One Flew Over the Cuckoo's Nest* (1975) was offered to Colleen Dewhurst, Anne Bancroft, Geraldine Page, and Angela Lansbury before Louise Fletcher accepted it. She won the Academy Award for Best Actress.

On the Beach

On the Beach, which starred Gregory Peck, Ava Gardner, and Fred Astaire, premiered simultaneously in major cities throughout the world on the same day—December 17, 1959—the first film to do so.

On the Waterfront

Frank Sinatra was director Elia Kazan's first choice to play Terry Malloy in *On the Waterfront.* The part ultimately went to Marlon Brando who won the Best Actor Award for his performance.

In the original filming of *On the Waterfront* (1954) Marlon Brando was to have died at the hands of the crooked union officers. When the Hays Office found out about the ending, a change was demanded stating that crime can not triumph in films. A new ending was shot, and Marlon Brando lived at the movie's end.

Three ex-heavyweight boxers played bit parts in *On the Waterfront.* All three, Tony Galento, Abe Simon, and Tami Mauriello, have fought Joe Louis. Galento was the only one of the three to knock Louis down.

Original names

Some fictional characters have undergone a name change. Mickey Mouse was originally to be Mortimer Mouse. Howdy Doody's original name was Elmer. Goofy was first known as Dippy Dawg. Bugs Bunny was first called Hap-

py Rabbit. Tom (of Tom and Jerry) was originally called Jasper.

Oscar nominations

Thelma Ritter and Deborah Kerr both
have been nominated six times for Academy
Awards, yet neither of them has ever won.
Richard Burton now holds the record for a performer with seven nominations but no Oscars.

Oscar—winning children

Children of Judy Garland, Kirk Douglas,
Ryan O'Neal, and Henry Fonda have all won
Oscars.

Maureen O'Sullivan

Maureen O'Sullivan's middle name is *Paul.*

Our Miss Brooks

Shirley Booth was first offered the role of
Constance Brooks on radio in *Our Miss Brooks.*
The role went to Eve Arden and brought her
even greater fame when the show was trans-
ferred to television.

The Outlaw

Howard Hughes's *The Outlaw,* featuring
the screen debut of both Jack Beutel and Jane
Russell, was actually completed in 1943 but
was not shown publicly until 1949 and was
officially distributed in 1950. This was due to

numerous censorship problems and the whims of Hughes. During that period of time Hughes spent several million dollars on advertisements. The film has never been shown on television.

"Over the Rainbow"

The song "Over the Rainbow" was almost eliminated from *The Wizard of Oz* (1939) because it was thought that it slowed down the movie.

Ozzie and Harriet

Before Ozzie and Harriet went on to fame as America's Favorite Young Couple on both radio and TV, Ozzie Nelson led his own orchestra with Harriet Hilliard as the lead singer.

P

Robert Paige

Universal's leading man Robert Paige once attended the U.S. Army Academy at West Point but quit before he graduated. His movie debut was in the 1935 movie *Annapolis Farewell*.

Jack Palance

Actor Jack Palance is responsible for Marlon Brando's broken nose, which Brando has never had reset. Palance accidentally hit Brando while playing around backstage. Palance had been Brando's understudy in the play *A Streetcar Named Desire* (1947).

Eugene Pallette

Rotund and burly character actor Eugene Pallette had two occupations not associated with his girth: he had been a jockey before his entry into films and served in the Air Corps during World War I.

Paramount

The mountain peak shown on the logo of Paramount films is one from the Wasatch mountains in Utah.

Barbara Parkins

Barbara Parkins teaches ballet when she is not acting.

Bert Parks

During World War II, Bert Parks served as a second lieutenant and was lost behind enemy lines in Burma for ten days. He entered the U.S. Army as a private in 1942 and was discharged in 1946 as a captain. He was awarded the Bronze Star.

Larry Parks

One of actor Larry Parks's legs was shorter than the other, caused by a childhood disease. He had to wear a special shoe for the shorter leg.

Michael Parks

Actor Michael Parks's "Long Lonesome Highway" made the top-twenty list of hit songs in 1970.

Estelle Parsons

Estelle Parsons, who won an Oscar for Best Supporting Actress for the 1967 movie *Bonnie and Clyde,* was once a hostess on *The Today Show* with Dave Garroway.

Lee Patrick–Elisha Cook, Jr.

Lee Patrick, who played Effie Perine, the secretary of Sam Spade (Humphrey Bogart) in *The Maltese Falcon* (1941), played the same role thirty-five years later for Sam Spade, Jr. (George Segal) in the 1976 movie *The Black Bird.* Elisha Cook, Jr., also repeated his role in the 1976 movie.

PATSY Awards

The first PATSY Awards were given out in 1951. Francis the Talking Mule was the first winner. Ronald Reagan served as emcee for the ceremonies.

Patton

Burt Lancaster was among many actors considered for the 1970 movie *Patton.* The title role was offered to Lee Marvin. John Wayne desperately wanted to play the role that George C. Scott bagged. Scott won the Best Actor Award for his performance.

For *Patton* George C. Scott shaved his head, wore false teeth, straightened his nose, and wore a mole. However, he did not alter his voice to try and match Patton's rather high voice.

General Omar Bradley received 10 percent of the profits of *Patton* for allowing Karl Malden to portray him.

Marisa Pavan

Italian actress Marisa Pavan, whose real name is Marisa Pierangeli, is the twin sister of the late actress Pier Angeli.

John Payne

John Payne bought the screen rights to Ian Fleming's James Bond novel *Moonraker* in 1954. It was turned down by the major studios over the years but was finally filmed and released in 1979.

Gregory Peck

Gregory Peck's father was a member of the University of Michigan's first basketball team in 1908-1909.

While he was a student at the University of California (Berkeley) Gregory Peck appeared in a production of *Moby Dick*. He played Starbuck. In 1956 he played Captain Ahab in a motion picture version of *Moby Dick*.

Gregory Peck was the first native Californian to win an Oscar—for his role as attorney Atticus Finch in the 1962 movie *To Kill a Mockingbird*— a startling fact considering that Oscars had been awarded for thirty-five years at that time.

Gregory Peck–Gary Cooper

Gregory Peck turned down the lead in the 1952 movie *High Noon*. Gary Cooper, who had turned down *Stagecoach* (1939), made *High Noon* and won the Academy Award for Best Actor. Peck's reason for turning the role down was that he felt he could not duplicate his good work in *The Gunfighter* (1950).

Gregory Peck–John Davidson–Brian Donlevy

Gregory Peck and John Davidson have both served as male models, Peck for Montgomery Ward and Davidson for Sears, Roebuck. Brian Donlevy modeled for illustrator Frank Lyendecker for Arrow shirts.

Gregory Peck–Larry Parks

Gregory Peck and Larry Parks both worked as tour guides at Radio City Music Hall at the same time. Peck also worked as a "talker" at the 1939 New York World's Fair.

Gregory Peck–Cliff Robertson

Actors Gregory Peck and Cliff Robertson, Academy Award winners for Best Actor, were both born in La Jolla, California.

Sam Peckinpah

Screenwriter/director Sam Peckinpah is the grandson of Denver S. Church, one of the three congressmen who voted against the entry of the United States in World War I.

Nat Pendleton

Character actor Nat Pendleton, nemesis of Abbott and Costello in several pictures, won a Silver Medal in wrestling at the 1920 Olympiad held in Antwerp. He could speak and write in five languages and held a degree in Economics from Columbia University.

George Peppard–Laurence Harvey

Actors George Peppard (Detroit, Michigan) and Laurence Harvey (Yonishkis, Lithuania) were both born on October 1, 1928.

Anthony Perkins

In 1957 Anthony Perkins made the record charts with the RCA Victor release "Moonlight Swim."

Jean Peters

While attending Ohio State University, former actress Jean Peters won a beauty contest. The prize was a screen test with 20th Century-Fox, which she passed.

Pete, the Pup

The ring around Pete's eye in the *Our Gang* shorts was painted on each time. The ring appeared around different eyes in the shorts.

Peter Pan

In 1953 when Walt Disney was creating the animated feature *Peter Pan,* he wanted to know what Tinkerbell should look like. Marilyn Monroe was then chosen as the model for the little fairy.

The Petrified Forest

Warner Bros. wanted Edward G. Robinson to play the part of Duke Mantee in the 1936 movie *The Petrified Forest,* but actor Leslie Howard refused to make the movie without Humphrey Bogart re-creating his Broadway role.

On February 8, 1943, Edward G. Robinson played Duke Mantee in *The Petrified Forest* on *Lux Radio Theater,* a part he almost played in the 1936 movie.

Humphrey Bogart's only television appearance was on the *Producer's Showcase* broadcast of May 30, 1955, on NBC. It was a presentation of *The Petrified Forest* with Lauren Bacall and Henry Fonda.

Penny Peyser

Actress Penny Peyser's father was a three-term Republican congressman.

Mackenzie Phillips

Mackenzie Phillips is the daughter of singer/composer John Phillips, former member of The Mamas and the Papas.

Mary Pickford

Mary Pickford made her acting debut in the play *The Warrens of Virginia* in 1908. The play was written by Cecil B. De Mille's brother, William.

America's Sweetheart, Mary Pickford, was made an honorary U.S. Army Colonel during World War I.

Picnic

For a scene in the 1955 movie *Picnic* William Holden had to have his chest hair shaved off to conform with the Motion Picture Code.

Walter Pidgeon

Walter Pidgeon began in show business as a singer and was the first person to record "What'll I Do," composed by Irving Berlin.

James Pierce

In 1928 James Pierce, who played Tarzan in *Tarzan and the Golden Lion* (1927), married Joan Burroughs, the daughter of Tarzan's creator. They played Tarzan and Jane on radio for 364 episodes.

Zasu Pitts

Zasu Pitts received her unusual first name from the last syllable of her Aunt Eliza and the first syllable of her Aunt Susan.

Zasu Pitts appeared in the first release prints of *All Quiet on the Western Front* (1930) as Paul Baumer's mother but she was replaced by Beryl Mercer. Miss Pitts had just appeared in a comedy and the studio executives felt that audiences would be more receptive to another actress. Whenever the preview audience saw Miss Pitts in a scene they began to laugh.

Planet of the Apes

Edward G. Robinson was to play the elderly scientist in the 1968 movie *Planet of the Apes* but because of his reaction to the makeup he was replaced by Maurice Evans.

Play Your Hunch

While he was host of TV's *Play Your Hunch* Merv Griffin carried Griffin Shoe Polish as a sponsor.

Donald Pleasance

English actor Donald Pleasance played the role of a POW in the 1963 movie *The Great Escape*. The role was a reminder of the twelve months that he actually spent as a prisoner of war when he was shot down over France during World War II.

George Plimpton

The father of "professional-amateur" George Plimpton, Francis Plimpton, was once deputy U.S. Representative to the United Nations.

Joan Plowright

Actress Joan Plowright played the daughter of Sir Laurence Olivier in the 1960 English movie *The Entertainer*. In actuality she is the wife of Olivier.

Christopher Plummer

Canadian actor Christopher Plummer's great-grandfather, Sir John Abbott, served once Prime Minister of Canada.

Walter Plunkett

Costume designer Walter Plunkett, who won an Oscar for his work on *An American in Paris* (1951), designed clothing for both the 1933 and 1949 versions of *Little Women* and for both the 1935 and 1948 versions of *The Three Musketeers*.

Sidney Poitier

Sidney Poitier was thirty-one years old when he played the delinquent high school student Gregory W. Miller in the 1955 movie *Blackboard Jungle*. His role was reversed years later when he played high school teacher Mr.

Braithwaite to a group of London delinquents in the 1967 movie *To Sir With Love*.

Michael J. Pollard

Michael J. Pollard (C.W. Moss in *Bonnie and Clyde*, 1967) was the first customer in the free give-away when the Beatles's Apple Boutique closed in London on July 31, 1968.

Carlo Ponti

In 1979 a Rome court found film producer Carlo Ponti guilty of illegally transferring money abroad. He was sentenced to four years in prison and fined $24,000,000. Because he and his actress wife Sophia Loren lived in France they are safe from extradition.

Jean Porter

Actress Jean Porter, ex-wife of Howard Hughes, authored the novel *Wake of the Devil*.

Tom Poston

During his youth actor Tom Poston was a professional acrobat with the Flying Zebleys troupe. He later boxed for a living.

Dick Powell–Jack Carson

Dick Powell (aged 58) and Jack Carson (aged 52), close friends, died of cancer on

January 2, 1963, within six hours of each other.

Jane Powell

At one time Jane Powell was the daughter-in-law of retired lightweight champion of the world Willie Ritchie.

Tyrone Power

During World War II Tyrone Power became a pilot in the Pacific. On one flight Lieutenant Power's passenger was author Edgar Rice Burroughs. Power was one of the first pilots to land on Iwo Jima shortly after the great battle there.

Tyrone Power, who died of a heart attack on November 16, 1958, shortly after filming an aggressive sword fight sequence on the set of *Solomon and Sheba,* was the son of actor Frederick Tyrone Power who was stricken by a fatal heart attack on December 30, 1931, at the Hollywood Athletic Club just a few hours after leaving the set of *The Miracle Man.*

Vincent Price, a friend of Tyrone Power, had a premonition of Power's death on the day that Power died.

Just prior to his fatal heart attack, Tyrone Power made a short film for the American Heart Association, warning of the risks of heart attack.

The Power of Love

Most trivia buffs believe that the first 3-D movie was *Bwana Devil,* released in 1952,

286

which starred Robert Stack. Actually the first 3-D movie in which the viewers had to wear glasses for a stereoscopic effect was made in 1922 and was titled *The Power of Love*. It ran five reels.

Otto Preminger

Film director Otto Preminger's father, Mark Preminger, held the position of Chief Prosecutor in Austria-Hungary, a position equal to that of the U.S. Attorney General. Otto and his father both received law degrees from the University of Vienna. Otto received his in 1928.

Paula Prentiss—Tommy Sands

Paula Prentiss and Tommy Sands were classmates at Lamar High School in Houston, Texas.

Presidential Descendants

Actor Wendell Corey was a descendant of U.S. Presidents John Adams and John Quincy Adams. William Holden and Martha Scott, the two leads in *Our Town* (1940), are both related to U.S. Presidents. Martha Scott's mother was a cousin of President William McKinley. William Holden's mother was a second cousin to President Warren G. Harding.

Robert Preston

At the age of fifteen, future actor Robert Preston joined a Shakespearean group coached by the mother of Tyrone Power.

Vincent Price

Vincent Price is a direct descendant of the first colonial child born in Massachusetts, Peregrine White.

Vincent Price's father, Vincent Leonard Price, was President of the National Candy Company.

On radio Vincent Price was one of three actors who played Simon Templar, star of *The Saint*. On television, the role was played by Roger Moore.

Vincent Price was once the art purchaser for Sears, Roebuck Company in Los Angeles.

Vincent Price–Edward G. Robinson

Vincent Price and Edward G. Robinson were both collectors and authorities on art. They appeared together in 1956 on the TV quiz show *The $64,000 Challenge* on the subject of art.

The Pride of the Yankees

In the filming of *The Pride of the Yankees* (1942) Gary Cooper, a righthander, portrayed first baseman Lou Gehrig, a lefthander. The scenes of Cooper batting left-handed were filmed with him swinging right-handed, the film was then reversed. Eddie Albert was briefly considered for the part of Lou Gehrig.

Pat Priest

Pat Priest, the second actress to play Marilyn Munster (Beverley Owen was the first) on the TV series *The Munsters*, is the daughter of Ivy Baker Priest, former Treasurer of the United States.

Roger Pryor–Meredith Wilson

Actor Roger Pryor was once a member of John Philip Sousa's marching band as a soloist; later he led his own band. Meredith Wilson, the creator of *The Music Man*, was also a soloist with the Sousa band.

Psycho

The building which served as the Bates's house in *Psycho* was only built to three-fourths scale.

In the classic shower scene in Hitchcock's *Psycho* (1960) the person wielding the knife was not Anthony Perkins, but his stand-in. Perkins was in New York when the scene was filmed.

Each time that *Psycho* was played on television Alfred Hitchcock received a batch of threatening letters from irate viewers.

PT 109

President John F. Kennedy wanted Warren Beatty to portray him in the 1963 movie *PT 109* although Cliff Robertson was selected to take the role, which also met with Kennedy's approval.

Bernard Punsley

Dead End Kid Bernard Punsley, who played the heavyset member Milty in films, is today a practicing physician in California.

The Purple Heart

Cedric Hardwicke and C. Aubrey Smith were originally planned as the Japanese judges for the 1944 movie *The Purple Heart*, but the makeup was not very convincing and they were replaced by Orientals.

Pygmalion

Clark Gable was not the first actor to use the word "damn" in a motion picture (*see* David O. Selznick). Leslie Howard uttered the word over and over in the 1938 version of *Pygmalion*. Lyle Talbot used the profanity even earlier in *The Thirteenth Guest* (1932).

Q

John Qualen

Character actor John Qualen received a proclamation in 1946 from King Haakon VII of Norway.

Anthony Quayle

Actor Anthony Quayle rose to the rank of major while serving with the Royal Artillery during World War II. He went on several secret missions for the British and the Americans. As a headquarters staff member at Gibraltar he had the opportunity to personally meet Winston Churchill, Dwight D. Eisenhower, and Charles de Gaulle. Quayle is the author of the novels *On Such a Night* and *Eight Hours from England.*

Queen Kelly

President John F. Kennedy's father, Joseph Kennedy, once invested $1 million in a movie that was never released. However, a portion of that film, *Queen Kelly*, starring Gloria Swanson and directed by Erich von Stroheim, was shown in the 1950 film *Sunset Boulevard.*

Juanita Quigley

Child star Juanita Quigley spent thirteen years in a convent as a Catholic nun after forsaking her Hollywood career in 1951.

Anthony Quinn

Actor Anthony Quinn was born in Mexico during the Revolution of 1915. His parents both fought on the side of Pancho Villa.

At the age of fourteen Anthony Quinn played saxophone in the Temple band at evangelist Aimée Semple McPherson's Los Angeles Four Square Temple.

Anthony Quinn was once turned down for a job as an usher at Grauman's Chinese Theatre. Today his footprints are among those of other celebrities who have left their mark in the cement in front of the famous Hollywood landmark.

As a teenager in Los Angeles, Anthony Quinn earned a few extra dollars as a sparring partner for heavyweight boxer Primo Carnera.

Anthony Quinn, who played the American pirate Jean Lafitte in the 1938 production of *The Buccaneer*, directed the 1958 version with Yul Brynner as Lafitte. Both movies were produced by Cecil B. De Mille, who was Quinn's father-in-law.

Quo Vadis?

Enrico Guazzoni's 1912 film version of *Quo Vadis?* was the first motion picture to run for two hours.

Elizabeth Taylor was vacationing in Europe in the same location that the film *Quo Vadis?* (1951) was being made, so just for fun she put on a robe and appeared in the movie as an extra. Sophia Loren also appeared in the film as an unbilled extra.

R

Race Drivers

Steve McQueen, James Garner, Dick Smothers, and Paul Newman are all professional race drivers in their spare time. The late James Dean also enjoyed racing.

George Raft

Actor George Raft's grandfather introduced the merry-go-round to the United States.

As a young boy George Raft was a mascot for the New York Highlanders baseball team. They later became the Yankees.

George Raft and underworld figure Benjamin "Bugsy" Siegel were boyhood friends in the Lower East Side of New York City. They maintained their friendship until Bugsy's murder in Virginia Hill's home on June 20 1947. The murder was never solved.

George Raft once won first place in a tango contest and was billed as "the fastest dancer in the world." Raft made his movie debut in *Taxi* (1932) as a dancer. James Cagney had convinced the studio to hire him because Raft could dance the Peabody so well.

George Raft turned down *Dead End* in 1937. He also turned down *High Sierra* and *The Maltese Falcon,* both released in 1941. Roles in all three of these films went to Humphrey Bogart. Raft turned down *High Sierra* because he did not want to be killed at the movie's end.

George Raft–Sam Ervin

Actor George Raft and retired Speaker of the House Sam Ervin share September 27, 1896, as their birthday.

George Raft–Al Jolson

In his youth, George Raft had been a professional boxer. Love for the ring led Raft, Eddie Mead, and Al Jolson to purchase the contract of boxer Henry Armstrong. Armstrong became the only man ever to hold three titles simultaneously: featherweight title (1937-1938), welterweight title (1938-1940), and the lightweight title (1938). It was the suggestion of his three owners that Armstrong fight for all three titles.

Douglas Rain

In the 1968 movie *2001: A Space Odyssey* the voice of HAL the computer was first recorded by actor Martin Balsam, but he was replaced by an English actor named Douglas Rain.

Ella Raines

Brigadier General Robin Olds, the husband of actress Ella Raines, once served as Commandant of the U.S. Air Force Academy.

Vera Hruba Ralston

Czech actress Vera Hruba Ralston competed in the 1936 Olympics held in Berlin and placed second to Sonja Henie in figure skating.

Sally Rand

The late Sally Rand appeared in the 1927 version of *King of Kings* as a servant to Mary Magdalene.

Tony Randall

Tony Randall played Reggie Yorke on the radio series *I Love a Mystery*.

Rasputin and the Empress

All three of the Barrymores, John, Ethel, and Lionel, appeared in the 1932 movie *Ras-*

putin and the Empress. It was their only movie appearance together.

Rasil Rathbone

Basil Rathbone was a descendant of King Henry IV on his mother's side.

During World War I Basil Rathbone, while serving as a captain with the Liverpool Scottish Regiment, was awarded the Military Cross.

Basil Rathbone, who was probably the best fencer among movie actors, won only one on-screen duel. The movie was *Romeo and Juliet* (1936).

Basil Rathbone was the host of the 1952 TV quiz show *Your Lucky Clue.*

Martha Raye

In the 1954 movie *A Star Is Born* Judy Garland sings about being born in a trunk in the Princess Theater in Pocatello, Idaho. Comedienne Martha Raye was born just that way, as Margaret Reed on August 27, 1916, in the backstage of a theatre in Butte, Montana. Her mother went back to performing in less than forty-eight hours.

Martha Raye was once a vocalist with Paul Ash's orchestra.

Martha Raye holds the rank of honorary lieutenant colonel in the Marine Corps and is also an honorary Green Beret. She has been wounded twice and is the only woman authorized to wear the Green Beret uniform.

Ronald Reagan

Future politician Ronald Reagan was student body president of his high school and also at Northwestern University.

Ronald Reagan claims to have saved seventy-seven people from drowning while serving as a lifeguard in 1926.

In the early 1930s Ronald Reagan was a radio announcer for the Chicago Cubs and the Chicago White Sox.

Captain Ronald Reagan signed Major Clark Gable's discharge papers in Culver City in June 1944.

Ronald Reagan—Hugh Marlowe

Ronald Reagan and Hugh Marlowe both worked at radio station WOC in Davenport, Iowa, at the same time in the 1930s.

Real Names

Sandra Dee's real name is Alexandra Zuck; British bombshell Diana Dors's real name is Diana Fluck; and Joanne Dru's real name is Joanne Laycock.

Rebecca

Part of the burning of Atlanta made for the 1939 movie *Gone With The Wind* was used in *Rebecca* (1940), in the burning of the town of Manderly scene.

Rebel Without a Cause

Warner Bros. originally wanted to film *Rebel Without a Cause* (1955) with Tab Hunter and Jayne Mansfield, but thanks to the insistence of director Nicholas Ray, James Dean and Natalie Wood were chosen instead.

Robert Redford

Robert Redford not only starred in the 1976 movie *All the President's Men* but he bought the movie's rights for $450,000 and produced it.

Robert Redford turned down the following roles:

1966	Nick	*Who's Afraid of Virginia Woolf?*
1967	Benjamin Braddock	*The Graduate*
1968	Guy Woodhouse	*Rosemary's Baby*
1970	Oliver Barrett IV	*Love Story*
1973	The Jackal	*The Day of the Jackal*

Robert Redford–Don Drysdale

Robert Redford and former pitcher Don Drysdale were classmates at Van Nuys High School.

Lynn Redgrave

Lynn Redgrave was confined to a wheelchair until she was six years old due to an acute case of anemia.

Lynn Redgrave—Vanessa Redgrave

Sisters Lynn and Vanessa Redgrave were both nominated for Best Actress in 1966, Lynn for her role in *Georgy Girl* and Vanessa for her role in *Morgan*. The Oscar that year went to Elizabeth Taylor for *Who's Afraid of Virginia Woolf?*

"Red River Valley"

"Red River Valley" was used as the theme song for two classic movies, *The Grapes of Wrath* (1940) and *The Ox-Bow Incident* (1943).

Rex Reed

Critic Rex Reed claims to be related to President Zachary Taylor and the Dalton Brothers.

George Reeves

George Reeves was miscredited in the screen credits of *Gone With The Wind* as playing the part of Brent Tarleton when he actually played the role of Stuart Tarleton, Brent's twin brother. Fred Crane played Brent Tarleton.

George Reeves appeared in a Signal Corps short titled *Sex Hygiene* in 1942, which was directed by none other than John Ford.

George Reeves, who appeared in 104 episodes as Superman, had been a Golden Gloves competitor in his youth and had his nose broken seven times.

Steve Reeves

Muscular actor Steve Reeves held the title of Mr. America in 1947.

Carl Reiner

During World War II Howard Morris was Carl Reiner's first sergeant in the U.S. Army.

Lee Remick

Actress Lee Remick was Edward R. Murrow's 500th guest on his TV program *Person to Person*.

Lee Remick got the female lead in the 1959 movie *Anatomy of a Murder* when Lana Turner walked out because she disliked the wardrobe.

Duncan Renaldo

Duncan Renaldo, best remembered for playing television's *Cisco Kid,* was once sent to prison for illegally entering the United States. The Rumanian-born actor spent eight months at McNeil Island and was freed when given a personal pardon by President Franklin D. Roosevelt.

A painting of an African queen by Duncan Renaldo was hung in the White House by Eleanor Roosevelt.

Michael Rennie

During World War II Michael Rennie served as a pilot with the RAF. He taught American pilots to fly in Georgia.

Tommy Rettig

Tommy Rettig, one of Lassie's several masters on the television show, was sentenced to five years in federal prison in 1975 for smuggling cocaine.

Anne Revere

Anne Revere, winner of the Best Supporting Actress Award for *National Velvet* (1944), claimed to be descended from Paul Revere.

Burt Reynolds

Burt Reynolds's father was Chief of Police in Riviera Beach, Florida.

Prior to becoming an actor, Burt Reynolds played football at Florida State University and was drafted by the Baltimore Colts. His football career ended prematurely when his knee was severely injured in an automobile accident. Reynolds wore jersey number 22 as a student at West Palm Beach High School and at Florida State University. He wore that number in the movies *The Longest Yard* (1974) and *Semi-Tough* (1977).

Burt Reynolds was the first person to pose nude for the centerfold of *Cosmopolitan* magazine (April 1972).

Debbie Reynolds

As a Girl Scout, actress Debbie Reynolds won forty-eight merit badges. She was Miss Burbank of 1948.

In 1957 Debbie Reynolds recorded the top-selling song of the year, "Tammy."

Debbie Reynolds–Marie McDonald

Harry Karl, the founder of Karl's Shoes, has been married to actresses Marie McDonald and Debbie Reynolds.

Gene Reynolds

Actor Gene Reynolds won an Oppie Award for the Best First Novel of 1972 with his book *The Truth About Unicorns*.

Richard III

The 1956 version of *Richard III* had the distinction of starring four actors who had been knighted: Sir Laurence Olivier, Sir John Gielgud, Sir Cedric Hardwicke, and Sir Ralph Richardson. The composer was also knighted, Sir William Walton.

Rin Tin Tin

Rin Tin Tin was voted the most popular film performer of 1926.

In the balloting for the Best Actor of 1927/ 1928 at the first Academy Awards ceremony Rin Tin Tin received the majority of the votes. He was eliminated by the judges, and thus German actor Emil Jannings became the first actor to win an Oscar for Best Actor.

Rio Rita

The first talkie filmed by RKO was *Rio Rita* in 1929. The film was begun in black and white and was finished in Technicolor.

Tex Ritter

Tex Ritter once ran, unsuccessfully, for the U.S. Senate in 1970.

To date Tex Ritter is the only person to be honored as a member of both the Cowboy Hall of Fame (located in Oklahoma City) and the Country and Western Music Hall of Fame (located in Nashville).

Thelma Ritter

Thelma Ritter once won a set of *Encyclopaedia Britannica* on the radio quiz show *Information Please*.

Joan Rivers

Comedienne/director Joan Rivers is the possessor of a Phi Beta Kappa key for her academic achievements at Barnard College.

"Road" Pictures

The "Road" pictures that did so much to make Bob Hope and Bing Crosby a star duo almost catapulted two other teams to superstardom. The series was first offered to George Burns and Gracie Allen. When they turned it down, Fred MacMurray and Jack Oakie were considered.

The Road Runner

In the 1951 Bugs Bunny cartoon *Operation: Rabbit*, Beep Beep the Road Runner, spoke for the first and last time.

Jason Robards, Jr.

Jason Robards, Jr., who appeared in the 1970 movie *Tora! Tora! Tora!*, about the Japanese bombing of Pearl Harbor on December 7, 1941, was actually there on the Day of Infamy. Robards was assigned to one of the naval vessels.

Jason Robards, Sr.

Jason Robards, Sr., played *Chandu the Magician* on radio.

The Robe

The Robe (1953) was the first Cinema-Scope movie brought to the screen.

Roberta

Lucille Ball played a mannequin in the 1935 Ginger Rogers/Fred Astaire movie *Roberta* made by RKO. Eventually Lucille Ball would own the entire studio.

Cliff Robertson

As a member of the Merchant Marines during World War II Cliff Robertson was assigned to the merchant ship *Admiral Cole*, which while serving in the Pacific Theater was bombed by Japanese planes.

Prior to making his movie debut in *Picnic* (1955), Cliff Robertson played Ranger Rod Brown on the 1953 children's TV show *Rod Brown of the Rocket Rangers*.

Cliff Robertson admitted publically that he sighted a UFO from his backyard for ten minutes one night in 1965.

On September 25, 1978, Cliff Robertson decided not to drive to the Los Angeles airport to catch a flight to San Diego. The flight he missed was PSA 182 which crashed that day and was, at the time, the worst aviation accident in U.S. history.

Willard Robertson

Character actor Willard Robertson was a practicing lawyer before becoming an actor with well over one hundred screen appearances to his credit.

Paul Robeson

Paul Robeson, the great black actor, once played football for Rutgers. He played so well that he became the first black football player to become an All-American. He was a four-letter man in college.

After graduating from Columbia University Paul Robeson was admitted to the New York Bar in 1923. His political views led to great controversial opinion about the actor, especially when he became the recipient of the Stalin Peace Prize.

Edward G. Robinson

Edward G. Robinson was shot to death at the end of *Little Caesar* (1931), *Silver Dollar* (1932), *I Love a Woman* (1933), *Barbary Coast* (1935), *Bullets or Ballots* (1936), and *Kid Galahad* (1937).

Jay Robinson

Character actor Jay Robinson once served fifteen months in a California prison in the early 1960s on a conviction of a narcotics arrest.

Sugar Ray Robinson

Ex-boxing champión Sugar Ray Robinson played bit parts in the 1968 movies *Candy* and *The Detective.*

Rochester

Eddie "Rochester" Anderson developed his rough, loud voice in his youth as a newspaper boy in San Francisco. Always trying to outshout the other paper boys, he eventually ruptured his vocal chords.

Rock, Rock, Rock

Connie Francis dubbed Tuesday Weld's singing voice in the 1956 musical *Rock, Rock, Rock*.

Rocky

Ken Norton was first considered for the part of Apollo Creed in the 1976 movie *Rocky*. The role was played by Carl Weathers.

Mortimer Rodgers

Doctor Mortimer Rodgers, the brother of composer Richard Rodgers, was at one time Tallulah Bankhead's personal physician.

Charles "Buddy" Rogers

America's Boyfriend, Charles "Buddy" Rogers, had his own orchestra in the 1930s in which he could play most of the instruments.

Ginger Rogers

Ginger Rogers's acting and singing mother, Lela, enlisted in the Marines under the name Lela Lelbrand. She was one of the first female Marines and rose to the rank of sergeant.

As a teenager in 1927 Ginger Rogers won first place in a Texas statewide Charleston contest. The trophy was presented by actor Dick Powell.

Ginger Rogers played Jean Harlow's mother in the 1965 movie *Harlow*. Miss Harlow's mother, who was a Christian Scientist, jeopardized her daughter's health in her waning days by refusing to permit her medical attention. Ginger Rogers is also a practicing Christian Scientist.

Will Rogers

Will Rogers was the first mayor (honorary) of Beverly Hills, California.

Ruth Roman–Betsy Drake

Ruth Roman and Cary Grant's third wife, Betsy Drake, were passengers on the *Andrea Doria* the fateful night that it was struck by the *Stockholm* (July 25, 1956).

Roman Holiday

Jean Simmons turned down *Roman Holiday* (1953). The part went to Audrey Hepburn who won the Oscar for Best Actress.

Mickey Rooney

In many films midgets have played the roles of small children. However, Mickey Rooney made his movie debut at age four playing a midget in *Not To Be Trusted* (1926).

In his youth, Mickey Rooney was the holder of the Pacific Southwest Junior Singles Championship in tennis. He once defeated Bill Tilden in five straight sets.

The role of Andy Hardy was to go to a young actor named Frankie Thomas. Mickey Rooney (5′ 3″) was picked because he was shorter than Ann Rutherford (5′ 3½″), his co-star.

Mickey Rooney composed the symphonic work "Melodante" which, in 1941, was performed by the Ford Symphony Orchestra.

Two of Mickey Rooney's eight wives have won beauty contests. Betty Jane Rase (number two) held the title of Miss Birmingham of 1944. Barbara Thomason (number five) was Miss Muscle Beach of 1954.

Mickey Rooney's son, Mickey, Jr., was one of the original members of the Mousketeers on TV's *The Mickey Mouse Club.*

Jimmy Roosevelt

President Franklin D. Roosevelt's son Jimmy was vice president under Samuel Goldwyn of Goldwyn Pictures beginning in 1939.

Billy Rose

At age fourteen, songwriter Billy Rose won first place in a high school shorthand and typing contest held at Madison Square Garden. In the 1919 U.S. National Shorthand Competition Championship he wrote shorthand with a potato in his writing hand, due to an injury he incurred the day before when he strained his wrist. Writing with the potato, in which a pen was placed, he won first place. He once exceeded 250 words a minute at a shorthand demonstration.

Rowan and Martin

In the early days of their act Dan Rowan was the comic foil and Dick Martin the straight man. They reversed their roles and success came their way.

Royal Wedding

Winston Churchill's daughter Sarah appeared in the 1951 film *Royal Wedding*, her only American movie appearance.

Harold Russell

Harold Russell is the only person to receive two Oscars for the same performance. He was nominated in the Best Supporting Actor category for *The Best Years of Our Lives* (1946) which he won. Academy officials also presented him with a Special Award. It was given to him by Shirley Temple.

Jane Russell

In 1946 an album of Jane Russell was released. It was titled *Let's Put Out the Lights*.

Jane Russell is the mother of several adopted children and the founder of the International Agency for the Adoption of Orphaned Children.

Kurt Russell

Kurt Russell, who portrayed Elvis Presley in the 1979 three-hour TV movie *Elvis*, actually began his movie career by debuting in the 1963 Elvis Presley movie *It Happened at the World's Fair* in a scene in which as a child he kicks Elvis in the shins.

Reb Russell

"B" Western star Reb Russell was quite an accomplished football player prior to turning his interest to films. In 1928 he was the All-American quarterback of the Big Six. He was also named an All-American fullback for Northwestern University. Knute Rockne called him the greatest line plunger of all time. His football accomplishments earned him a spot in Robert L. Ripley's "Believe It Or Not!" column.

Rosalind Russell

Rosalind Russell was given her first name by her parents after the name of a ship on which they once vacationed, the *Rosalind*.

Rosalind Russell worked for a short time as a model for Saks Fifth Avenue.

Rosalind Russell wrote the screenplay for the 1957 movie *The Unguarded Moment* which starred Esther Williams in a nonswimming role.

Rosalind Russell became actress Pat Morrow's mother-in-law upon Pat's marriage to her son Lance.

Russian

Before the French government would let the 1939 version of the movie *Beau Geste* be viewed in France, Columbia Pictures had to make the villain a Russian.

Russian-born

Al Jolson, Irving Berlin, and George Sanders were all born in Russia.

Ann Rutherford

Ann Rutherford's father, John Guilberty Rutherford, was a Metropolitan Opera singer. Her mother, Lucille Mansfield, was an actress in silent films.

Irene Ryan

In the TV series *The Beverly Hillbillies*, Granny was Jed's mother-in-law, but in real life Irene Ryan (Granny) was only five years older than Buddy Ebsen (Jed).

Robert Ryan

While at Dartmouth College in 1931, Robert Ryan won first prize in a playwriting contest.

Robert Ryan was Nelson Rockefeller's fraternity brother at Dartmouth.

Mark Rydell

Mark Rydell was an actor in the 1959 TV soap *As the World Turns* before stepping behind the camera to direct such movies as *The Reivers* (1969), *The Cowboys* (1972), and *Cinderella Liberty* (1973).

S

Sabrina

Cary Grant backed out of an agreement to do *Sabrina* (1954) and was replaced by Humphrey Bogart. Grant had been the choice of director Billy Wilder.

Sacheen Littlefeather

Sacheen Littlefeather, the Indian girl who refused Marlon Brando's Oscar for *The Godfather* (1972) for him, once was named Miss American Vampire under her stage name of Maria Cruz.

George Sanders

George Sanders was the younger brother

of actor Tom Conway, and both played *The Falcon* in films.

George Sanders was married to both Zsa Zsa Gabor and her sister Magda Gabor.

Sands of Iwo Jima

Kirk Douglas was briefly considered for the part of Sergeant Stryker in *Sands of Iwo Jima* (1949). The role went to John Wayne who was nominated for the Best Actor Award.

Rene A. Gagnon, Ira H. Hayes, and John H. Bradley, three of the original six Marines who raised the flag on Mount Suribachi, portrayed themselves in *Sands of Iwo Jima*. The other three had been killed on the island.

Santana

Actors Humphrey Bogart and Ray Milland both owned boats named *Santana*. Bogart bought his from Dick Powell for $55,000.

Sarah Siddons Award

The famed Sarah Siddons Award, given annually for the best theatrical performance in Chicago, was named for the British theatre's Queen of Tragedy. The actual award came into being after it was fictitiously used in the 1950 movie *All About Eve*.

Saratoga

Jean Harlow died during production of the 1937 movie *Saratoga*. A stand-in, Mary

Dees, completed her scenes while Paula Winslowe dubbed her voice.

Alvin Sargent

Alvin Sargent, one of the soldiers who is machine-gunned by a Japanese Zero at Schofield Barracks in the 1953 movie *From Here to Eternity,* wrote the screenplay for the 1977 movie *Julia.*

Telly Savalas

Christina Kapsallis Savalas, mother of actor Telly Savalas, is a former Miss Greece.

In the early 1950s Aristotle "Telly" Savalas hosted a talk show on the U.S. government radio program *Voice of America* on which he interviewed celebrities.

Telly Savalas has a master's degree in psychology.

Sayonara—West Side Story

In two movies the actor and actress who played lovers each won an Oscar in a supporting role. The first time came in 1957 when Red Buttons and Miyoshi Umeki won for *Sayonara.* The second occasion came in 1961 when George Chakiris and Rita Moreno won for *West Side Story.*

Scarface

Jack LaRue was originally set to play the coin-flipping hood in *Scarface* (1932) but was replaced by George Raft.

Ever wonder what denomination of coin George Raft flipped in *Scarface?* Raft claimed it was only a nickel.

Scent of Mystery

Smell-O-Vision, where actual scents were released inside a theater, was introduced in the 1959 movie *Scent of Mystery.* It was created by Michael Todd, Jr.

Maximilian Schell

One of the great-grandfathers of Maximilian Schell was the court composer and a close friend of Franz Liszt and Richard Wagner (Liszt's father-in-law).

Ernest B. Schoedsack

Movie producer Ernest B. Schoedsack (*King Kong,* 1933) was a combat photographer in the Signal Corps during World War I.

Stuart Schulberg

Producer Stuart Schulberg is the brother of Budd Schulberg, author of *On the Waterfront* and *What Makes Sammy Run.* The title of the movie *On the Waterfront* (1954) was originally *Waterfront,* but was changed due to a conflict with a television series of the same name. Stuart and Budd's father, Benjamin P. Schulberg, was chief of productions at Paramount.

Paul Scofield

Paul Scofield, who won the Best Actor Award for the 1966 movie *A Man for All Seasons*, played Juliet in his school production of *Romeo and Juliet*.

Devon Scott

Actress Devon Scott, daughter of George C. Scott, was once the roommate of Caroline Kennedy at Vassar.

Randolph Scott

Randolph Scott, a native Virginian, was Gary Cooper's dialogue coach for the 1929 version of *The Virginian*.

Zachary Scott

Zachary Scott's father was a one-time president of the National Tuberculosis Society.

Scrooge

The 1970 movie *Scrooge* was originally planned to star Richard Harris. That deal fell through, and Rex Harrison was then considered. The part finally went to Albert Finney.

Sea Fury

Sea Fury was Victor McLaglen's last picture. It was released on November 7, 1959.

That same day McLaglen died of heart failure at the age of seventy-three.

The Sea Wolf

In filming the seventh version of Jack London's *The Sea Wolf* (1958), the schooner used in the movie as Wolf Larsen's *Ghost* was actor Sterling Hayden's vessel, the *Gracie S.*

Sears, Roebuck Company

Lauren Bacall, Susan Hayward, Ginger Rogers, and Gloria Swanson have all posed as models for the Sears, Roebuck Company catalogue.

George Seaton

George Seaton, long-time successful writer, director, and producer, who was responsible for such films as *The Song of Bernadette* (1943) as writer, *Miracle on 34th Street* (1947) for which he won an Oscar for Best Screenplay, and *Airport* (1970) as writer/director, was also the first man to play the Lone Ranger on radio when it debuted on January 30, 1933, on Detroit radio station WXYZ.

The Secret Six

Clark Gable and Jean Harlow made six movies together; the first movie was titled *The Secret Six* in 1931. Ralph Bellamy made his screen debut in the film.

Erich Segal

Erich Segal, author of *Love Story* (1970) is an active marathon runner who once ran the 26 miles, 385 yards of the Boston Marathon with a seven-pound tape recorder on his back to record his activities.

George Segal

During his collegiate and later his military days, George Segal played banjo and sang with a jazz band.

Peter Sellers

Peter Sellers was the vice president of the London Judo Society.

David O. Selznick

David O. Selznick was ordered to pay $5,000 as a fine to the MPPA (Motion Picture Producers Association) for the use of the profanity "damn" in *Gone With The Wind* (1939).

Rod Serling

During his service with the U.S. Army in World War II actor Rod Serling won seventeen of eighteen amateur boxing matches.

Rod Serling was the first creative writer to win the Peabody Award. His brother Robert authored the novel *The President's Plane is Missing,* which was made into a 1973 TV movie.

The Seven Samurai–Yojimbo

Two of director Akira Kurosawa's Japanese films were made into successful Westerns. *The Seven Samurai* (1954) became *The Magnificent Seven* (1960). *Yojimbo* (1961) became *A Fistful of Dollars* (1964).

Shamus

Morris, the finicky cat on television's 9-Lives cat food commercials, appeared with Burt Reynolds in the 1973 movie *Shamus*. His real name was Lucky (he received his name when he was rescued from the animal shelter). The first Morris died in 1978.

Omar Sharif

Omar Sharif was born in Alexandria, Egypt, and is the only prominent world famous Egyptian actor. He is a Life Master in bridge.

Omar Sharif's second movie appearance was in the 1953 Egyptian movie *The Blazing Sun*, which showed the first kiss in an Arabic movie.

Douglas Shearer

Winner of twelve Academy Awards, Douglas Shearer was the brother of Oscar-winning actress Norma Shearer and the brother-in-law of Irving Thalberg.

Norma Shearer

In her youth Norma Shearer posed for noted artists James Montgomery Flagg and Charles Dana Gibson.

Norma Shearer, nicknamed by MGM as "First Lady of the Screen," was introduced to the picture world as a piano player in a Montreal nickelodeon. She was the wife of movie mogul Irving Thalberg, "Hollywood's Boy Wonder."

Robert Shaw

The late Robert Shaw was the author of the prize-winning novel *The Sun Doctor* (1962 Hawthornden Prize) and the play *The Man in the Glass Booth*.

Sherlock Holmes

Although the line has been perpetuated in countless films, the words "Elementary, my dear Watson" do not appear in any of Arthur Conan Doyle's stories about Sherlock Holmes. The closest approximation is in the story *The Crooked Man* when Watson says "Excellent" and Holmes replies "Elementary."

Arthur Shields

Character actor Arthur Shields was the younger brother of Barry Fitzgerald. Shields was the family name.

Brooke Shields

Actress and model Brooke Shields was once the Ivory Snow baby.

Show Boat

All the tunes in the movie *Show Boat* (1936 and 1951), except for one, were composed by Oscar Hammerstein II and Jerome Kern. The exception was "Bill" which was composed by P. G. (Pelham Grenville) Wodehouse, the famous writer.

Don Siegel

Director Don Siegel has made cameo appearances in several of his movies: *Edge of Eternity* (1959) as a man at a motel pool; *The Killers* (1964) as a man cooking hamburger in a diner; *Coogan's Bluff* (1968) as a man in an elevator; and *Dirty Harry* (1971) as a man running down the street. He even played a bartender in the movie *Play Misty for Me* (1971), directed by Clint Eastwood.

Simone Signoret

French actress Simone Signoret's father served as chief interpretor in the League of Nations and later for the United Nations.

Silent Movie

Mel Brooks got friends Burt Reynolds, James Caan, Liza Minnelli, and Paul Newman to appear in his 1976 film *Silent Movie* for union-scale wages.

Henry Silva

Cindy Conway, who in 1959 married actor Henry Silva, is a former "Miss Canada" beauty contest winner.

The Silver Chalice

The Silver Chalice (1954) was Paul Newman's first movie. Newman thought his acting was so bad in the film that he took out an advertisement in a Los Angeles paper to apologize for what he believed was a poor performance.

Jay Silverheels

Jay Silverheels, a Mohawk Indian who appeared in many Westerns but is better known as the Lone Ranger's Indian companion Tonto on television, was at one time a professional lacrosse player in his native country of Canada. He was also a runner-up for the U.S. National Golden Gloves middleweight championship.

After retiring from acting, Jay Silverheels participated in harness racing professionally.

Phil Silvers

In his youth Phil Silvers spent time in a reform school. He had been a member of a street gang called the Bronzes.

Frank Sinatra

When Francis Albert Sinatra was born on December 12, 1915, he weighed 13½ pounds.

Frank Sinatra once saved the life of a three-year-old lad named Duke Jones when the boy fell from a wharf into the ocean at Long Beach Harbor. Sinatra plunged into the water and brought the child to the surface.

Frank Sinatra–Marlon Brando

The sons of both Frank Sinatra and Marlon Brando have been kidnapped. Each was safely returned to their fathers (Frank, Jr., in 1964, Christian Brando in 1972).

Penny Singleton

Penny Singleton got the role of Blondie in that movie series when actress Shirley Deane became ill. Miss Singleton had to bleach her brunette hair for the part.

Penny Singleton supplied the voice of Jane on the animated cartoon series *The Jetsons*.

The Sisters

Three different endings were filmed for the 1938 Errol Flynn–Bette Davis movie *The Sisters*. Preview audiences determined the ending that was finally used.

Red Skelton

Comedian Red Skelton's father, Joseph Skelton, was not only a clown with the Hagenbeck and Wallace Circus but was also a practicing lawyer and teacher. Red's father unfortunately died before Richard "Red" Skelton was born.

Red Skelton has composed over sixty symphonies that have been performed by the London Philharmonic and pianist Van Cliburn.

Spyros Skouras

Spyros Skouras, one-time head man of 20th Century-Fox studios, was born in the town of Skourahorion, Greece. He was offered the ambassadorship to Greece on four different occasions, by two U.S. Presidents. He turned down the offers.

Walter Slezak

Actor Walter Slezak has been depicted on a postage stamp in Austria, his country of birth.

Walter Slezak's daughter Erika played Victoria Lord Riley on the television soap *One Life to Live*.

Darwood Smith

Darwood Smith, who played Waldo in the *Our Gang* films, is today an Elder in the Seventh Day Adventist Church. He earned a master's degree in theology while attending Michigan State.

Gladys Smith

Actresses Mary Pickford and Alexis Smith shared the same real name—Gladys Smith.

Kate Smith

Kate Smith was the first private citizen to be given the American Red Cross Medal of Valor. She was also made an honorary Texas Ranger.

In 1958 Kate Smith wrote the *Company's Coming Cookbook*.

Smithsonian Institution

The original armchairs used by Archie (Carroll O'Connor) and Edith (Jean Stapleton) on *All in the Family* were donated to the Smithsonian Institution in the summer of 1978.

Soap operas

The brothers and sisters of many prominent show business personalities have appeared on the daily TV soap operas. Georganne La Piere, sister of Cher, was on *General Hospital*. Frances Heflin, sister of Van Heflin, was on *All My Children*. Irene Dailey, sister of Dan Dailey, was on *Another World*. Gail Brown, sister of actress Karen Black, also appeared on *Another World*. Joan Copeland, sister of playwright Arthur Miller, appeared on *Search for Tomorrow* and *Love of Life*. Ed Nelson's son Chris appears on *General Hospital* as does Kin Shriner, son of comedian Herb Shriner. Stuart Whitman's younger brother, Kipp Whitman, appeared on both *The Edge of Night* and *As the World Turns*. Nick Benedict, who is a regular on *All My Children,* is the son of director

Richard Benedict. Loretta Young's sister, Judy Lewis, was on *The Secret Storm*. Marlon Brando's sister Jocelyn was on *Love of Life*.

Many movie actors and actresses have appeared on soaps. Robert Alda, the father of Alan Alda, played on the TV serial *Love of Life*. Barry Newman played John Barnes on *The Edge of Night*. Hal Holbrook and Patty Duke both worked on *The Brighter Day*. Dyan Cannon played on both *For Better or Worse* and *Full Circle*. Joan Bennett appeared on *Dark Shadows*. Dana Andrews has been on *Bright Promise*. Efrem Zimbalist, Jr., appeared on *Concerning Miss Marlowe*. Glenn Corbett appeared on *The Doctors,* Mamie Van Doren on *General Hospital,* Troy Donahue on *The Secret Storm,* Ruby Dee on *The Guiding Light* and *Peyton Place,* Ruth Warrick on *All My Children,* and James Earl Jones on *The Guiding Light*. Christopher (*Superman*) Reeve appeared on *Love of Life,* Barbara Britton on *Date With Life,* Ann Sheridan on *Another World,* and Walter Slezak on *One Life To Live,* playing his daughter's (Erika Slezak) godfather.

The following actors and actresses have appeared on *Search for Tomorrow:* George Maharis, Ross Martin, Sandy Duncan, Don Knotts, Tom Ewell, Jill Clayburgh, Lee Grant, and Roy Scheider.

Something's Got To Give

At the time of her death (1962), Marilyn Monroe was working on a film titled *Some-*

thing's Got To Give. It was later retitled *Move Over Darling* (1963) and starred Doris Day.

Elke Sommer

In 1959 eighteen-year-old Elke Schletz (Elke Sommer) won the Miss Viareggio, Italy, beauty contest.

Gale Sondergaard

Gale Sondergaard was the first Academy Award-winning actress (Best Supporting Actress for *Anthony Adverse,* 1936) to appear in a soap opera—TV's *The Best of Everything.*

Sons-in-law Among Producers and Directors

James Franciscus: son-in-law of William Wellman
Bob Livingston: son-in-law of Hal Roach
Arthur Lowe: son-in-law of Adolph Zukor
William Orr: son-in-law of Jack Warner
Anthony Quinn: son-in-law of Cecil B. De Mille
Milton Sperling: son-in-law of Jack Warner
Mervyn LeRoy, Charles Victor, and Billy Rose were all sons-in-law of Jack Warner, all having married his daughter Doris.

Son of Kong

Son of Kong was the first sequel movie to be released the same year as the original, *King Kong* (1933).

Ann Sothern

As a high school student Ann Sothern won prizes for her musical compositions. Once she represented the state of Minnesota in a youthful composer competition held in Detroit.

Ann Sothern–Veronica Lake

Ann Sothern's real name is Harriette Lake. Veronica Lake's real name was Constance Frances Marie Ockelman.

David Soul

Actor/singer David Soul was once signed by the Chicago White Sox.

The Sound of Music

Mrs. Myra Franklin of Cardiff, Wales has seen *The Sound of Music* (1965) over 900 times. A Korean television station once aired the movie deleting all the musical numbers.

South Pacific

Among those considered for the part of Nellie Forbush in the 1958 movie *South Pacific* were Elizabeth Taylor and Mary Martin, who played the part on Broadway. The role went to Mitzi Gaynor.

Spaghetti Westerns

A Fistful of Dollars, For a Few Dollars More, and *The Good The Bad and The Ugly* are Italian-made Westerns, based on Japanese stories, filmed in Spain, with an American star.

Spellbound

Alfred Hitchcock's 1945 movie *Spellbound* was filmed in black and white, but a single scene of a gun being fired showed the color red for one-twelfth of a second.

Mickey Spillane

Author Mickey Spillane (Frank Morrison Spillane), creator of detective Mike Hammer, trained pilots in World War II, flew several combat missions, and previous to that performed in a circus on the trampoline. He also drew for comic books such as *Plastic Man* before writing detective stories.

Mike Hammer has been played in the movies by Biff Eliot, Ralph Meeker, and Robert Bray. Darren McGavin played the role on television. Mickey Spillane played his own creation in the 1963 movie *The Girl Hunters*.

The Spirit of St. Louis

A young, unknown actor named Clint Eastwood was originally considered for the role of aviator Charles Lindbergh in the 1957 movie *The Spirit of St. Louis*. However, since Eastwood was an unknown, James Stewart, then forty-nine, won the part of the twenty-five-year-old flyer.

Kay Spreckles

Kay Spreckles, Clark Gable's fifth wife and the mother of his only child, John Clark Gable, Jr., appeared with her then-future husband in the 1939 movie *Idiot's Delight* as an un-credited chorus girl.

Robert Stack

Robert Stack's father, James Stack, is credited with coining the term "The Beer That Made Milwaukee Famous."

Robert Stack's brother, James, Jr., is a millionaire in his own right. He was once married to actress Wanda Hendrix.

Robert Stack was a skeet-shooting champion in 1937 and once held the world's record of 351 consecutive hits.

Stagecoach

Director John Ford asked John Wayne to read the part of the Ringo Kid in *Stagecoach* (1939). Wayne then suggested Lloyd Nolan for the role that was to catapult him to stardom.

Norman Rockwell painted the characters used in the credits for the 1966 version of *Stagecoach*. Wayne Newton sang the film's theme song.

Sylvester Stallone

Sylvester Stallone appeared in an episode of *Police Story* in 1975 in which he played a cop named Elmore Quincy Caddo. In one scene he asked his partner to call him by his nickname—Rocky. This was over a year before Stallone's 1976 hit movie *Rocky*.

Sylvester Stallone, former lion cage cleaner, had only $106.00 in his bank account when he sold the screenplay for *Rocky*.

Lionel Stander

Character actor Lionel Stander was a Wall Street broker before becoming an actor. He was one of the many performers blacklisted in the 1950s.

Barbara Stanwyck

Ruby Stevens received her stage name of Barbara Stanwyck when Willard Mack named her after a character called Jane Stanwyck in the English play *Barbara Frietchie*.

Barbara Stanwyck is a member of the National Cowboy Hall of Fame.

A Star Is Born (1954)

In 1942, almost twelve years before her screen portrayal, Judy Garland was in a performance of *A Star Is Born* on radio. Her radio co-star was Walter Pidgeon.

For the Norman Maine role in 1954's *A Star Is Born* Marlon Brando, Henry Fonda, and Cary Grant were considered. The part went to James Mason.

In the 1954 version of *A Star Is Born* a drunk asks Judy Garland to sing "Melancholy Baby." The actor playing the drunk was an extra, but his dubbed voice was that of Humphrey Bogart.

Charles Starrett

Western actor Charles Starrett played football at Dartmouth College in his collegiate days. His first movie appearance was in 1926 when he played himself as a professional football player in the film *The Quarterback*.

Star Trek

The voice of the computer on the television series *Star Trek* was Majel Barrett, who also played Nurse Christine Chapel. Her husband is *Star Trek*'s creator/producer, Gene Roddenberry.

Paramount studio gave an eleven-foot model of the *U.S.S. Enterprise* from TV's *Star Trek* to the Smithsonian Institution for a temporary exhibit. It is now on display in the Life in the Universe Gallery of the National Air and Space Museum.

Rod Steiger

Rod Steiger, long noted for playing elderly roles, is the same age as Paul Newman and a year younger than Marlon Brando, yet in the 1954 movie *On the Waterfront* he played Brando's older brother.

Stella Award

The British equivalent to the Academy Award is called the Stella Award.

Andrew Stevens

Actor Andrew Stevens is the son of actress Stella Stevens and is married to Kate Jackson. He played the lead role in the 1978 TV movie *The Bastard*.

George Stevens

Landers Stevens, father of George Stevens, played the father of Betty Furness in *Swing Time* (1936), which was directed by George Stevens.

Stella Stevens

Actress Stella Stevens was the *Playboy* Playmate centerfold in the January 1960 issue.

James Stewart

James Stewart, a graduate of Princeton University, still owns every hat he has worn in his films since his movie debut in *The Murder Man* (1935). He has also worn the same pair of shoes in his last two dozen films.

In the 1952 movie *The Greatest Show on Earth* James Stewart's face is never seen, for he always has clown makeup over it.

James Stewart retired with the rank of

brigadier general in 1968 after twenty-seven years in the Air Force Reserve. At that time he was awarded the Distinguished Service Medal, only the second time that the Award was bestowed on a reserve officer. During World War II Stewart flew twenty combat missions.

James Stewart–Jose Ferrer

In his youth James Stewart recorded one side of a record titled "Love Comes But Once" backed up by the college band of José Ferrer called the Pied Pipers. The flip side was of Ferrer singing "Sweet Georgia Brown."

St. Genesius

St. Genesius is the patron saint of actors. Robert Preston still wears the medal of St. Genesius given to him by actress Barbara Stanwyck.

The Sting

Famed gambling expert John Scarne made a brief appearance of sorts in the 1973 movie *The Sting*. It was Scarne's hands, not those of Paul Newman, doing the fancy card-manipulating in the classic poker scene.

Fuzzy St. John

Western sidekick and comedian Al "Fuzzy" St. John was the cousin of Roscoe "Fatty" Arbuckle.

Edmund Stoiber

During a burglary in his home actor Edmund Stoiber was shot in the neck where today the bullet is still lodged. After recovery, the first two roles he played on television were those of robbery victims.

Lewis Stone

Three of the aunts of actor Lewis Stone were the founders of the Boston Opera Company.

A record was set by actor Lewis Stone who, as a contract player, signed with MGM for twenty-nine consecutive years.

Barbra Streisand

Barbra Streisand was nominated for a Tony for her first Broadway play, *I Can Get It for You Wholesale*. She won a Grammy for her first record album, *The Barbra Streisand Album* (1963). She won an Emmy for her first TV special, *Color Me Barbra* (1965). She won an Oscar for her first movie, *Funny Girl* (1967). She has twice been selected for the International Best Dressed List and in 1977 she won another Oscar with Paul Williams for Best Song, "Evergreen," from *A Star Is Born* (1976).

Barbra Streisand–Neil Diamond

Singers Barbra Streisand and Neil Diamond attended the same high school, Erasmus

High School in Brooklyn, New York. They sang in the school choir.

Woody Strode

Character actor Woodrow "Woody" Strode, who appeared in *The Buccaneer* (1958) and *The Man Who Shot Liberty Valance* (1962) and who also played the title role in *Sergeant Rutledge* (1960), was formerly a football player with the Los Angeles Rams.

Sally Struthers

Sally Struthers provided the voice of Pebbles on the *Pebbles and Bamm Bamm Show* on television.

Margaret Sullavan

Margaret Sullavan made her movie debut in the 1933 film *Only Yesterday* which had been turned down by Claudette Colbert and Irene Dunne.

Barry Sullivan

Actor Barry Sullivan is the father-in-law of musician Jim Messina (of Loggins and Messina).

Ed Sullivan

At Port Chester High School in New York state, Ed Sullivan received ten athletic letters for basketball, baseball, and football. He was later captain of a championship semi-pro basketball team.

The total budget for Ed Sullivan's first show on June 20, 1948, was under $1,500. Among the guests were Eugene List, Richard Rodgers, Oscar Hammerstein II, Ruby Goldstein, and a new comedy team—Dean Martin and Jerry Lewis.

Sunset Boulevard

For the part of Norma Desmond in the 1950 classic *Sunset Boulevard,* co-writer and director Billy Wilder originally wanted Mae West or Mary Pickford. The part went to Gloria Swanson who won a Best Actress nomination.

A suitable mansion on Sunset Boulevard could not be found for the movie *Sunset Boulevard,* so a mansion on Wilshire Boulevard, which belonged to J. Paul Getty, was used. The same house was used in the 1955 movie *Rebel Without a Cause.*

Most people are familiar with the opening sequence of *Sunset Boulevard* which shows William Holden floating face down in a swimming pool. What most people do not know is that the studio originally planned and filmed a tracking shot through rows of corpses in a morgue where Holden's body sat up and addressed the audience. The scene was not used.

The Sunshine Boys

Jack Benny was first cast to play opposite Walter Matthau in the Neil Simon movie *The*

Sunshine Boys (1975) but was replaced by George Burns. Benny's death in December 1974 gave Burns the role that was to turn his career around. Burns won the Best Supporting Actor Award.

Jacqueline Susann

Prior to becoming a best-selling author Jacqueline Susann did TV commercials and appeared on Broadway with Eddie Cantor in the play *Banjo Eyes*.

Jacqueline Susann appeared in a cameo role as a reporter in the 1967 movie *Valley of the Dolls*, which was based on her highly successful novel.

Frank Sutton

Frank Sutton, who played Marine sergeant Vince Carter on television's *Gomer Pyle USMC*, actually served as a sergeant in the U.S. Army during World War II.

Gloria Swanson

In her seventies Gloria Swanson began a new career as a sculptress, with her works being put on exhibition at the Hamilton Gallery in London in 1979.

The Swarm

While filming the 1978 movie *The Swarm*, producer Irwin Allen insured his crew for $70 million against insect bites. Lloyds of London carried the policy.

T

Lyle Talbot

Character actor Lyle Talbot's real name is Lysle Henderson. The last name of the aunt who adopted him was Hollywood, hence came the story that Talbot's real name was Lyle Hollywood.

Tall in the Saddle

The screenplay for *Tall in the Saddle* (1944) which starred John Wayne was written by actor Paul Fix.

Mark Tapscott

On the TV soap *Days of Our Lives* Bob Anderson, played by Mark Tapscott, was to have a heart attack on the show. The day prior to the filming Tapscott actually experienced a heart attack.

Tarzan

All of the following actors were considered for the role of Tarzan in the 1932 version of *Tarzan the Ape Man:* Charles Bickford, Johnny Mack Brown, Clark Gable, Joel McCrea, Tom Tyler, Herman Brix (Bruce Bennett), Buster Crabbe, and Glenn Morris.

Four movie Tarzans were Olympians: Johnny Weissmuller, Herman Brix, Buster Crabbe, and Glenn Morris.

A Tarzan yell was first given in the 1929 serial *Tarzan the Tiger* by Frank Merrill.

Elizabeth Taylor

Although Elizabeth Taylor was born outside of London on February 27, 1932, she was an American citizen at birth because both of her parents were American-born.

At the age of fourteen Elizabeth Taylor had a book published titled *Nibbles and Me,* about her pet chipmunk. That same year she sold a water color landscape to a greeting card company.

Elizabeth Taylor was made an honorary lieutenant-colonel of Florida at age seventeen. Later she was named an honorary colonel of Kentucky at age twenty-four.

When the *Harvard Lampoon* conferred

upon Elizabeth Taylor the year's Worst Actress Award in 1950 for *The Conspirators*, Miss Taylor actually went to Harvard to receive the award.

Two of Elizabeth Taylor's weddings have occurred on February 21: in 1952 to Michael Wilding and in 1957 to Mike Todd.

Elizabeth Taylor converted to the Jewish faith in 1959. For twenty years her films were banned in Arab countries. The ban was lifted in September 1979.

Elizabeth Taylor is the only known survivor of a rare type of staphylococcus pneumonia which she nearly died from in 1961.

Elizabeth Taylor appeared on more covers (eleven) of *Life* magazine than any other person.

Robert Taylor

While in high school Robert Taylor won the Nebraska State Oratorical Championship of 1929.

While a student at Pomona College Robert Taylor played cello in the school orchestra.

When Robert Taylor signed his first Hollywood contract in 1934 he became the lowest-paid contract actor in Hollywood's history. He signed a seven-year contract for $35 a week. In 1936 his salary went to $50 a week and went up substantially from there, but only because of the generosity of MGM, the studio.

Robert Taylor was awarded the title Outdoorsman of the Year in 1954, as recipient of the first Winchester Award.

Tea for Two

As a young lady, Doris Day rebroke her leg dancing to the song "Tea for Two" while listening to the radio. She had previously broken it in an auto accident. In 1950 she starred in the musical *Tea for Two*. Doctors had believed she would never be able to walk again. Needless to say she proved them wrong.

Teenagers

Three young actors who were on successful television series during the sixties had each appeared in cheap sci-fi "teenage" movies in the fifties. They were Gary Conway, *I Was a Teenage Frankenstein* (1957); Michael Landon, *I Was a Teenage Werewolf* (1957); and Robert Vaughn, *Teenage Caveman* (1958). The TV series involved were *Burke's Law, Bonanza,* and *The Man from U.N.C.L.E.*, respectively.

Shirley Temple

Shirley Temple was the youngest person ever to have an entry in *Who's Who*. She was also the youngest person ever to appear on the cover of *Time* magazine (April 1936).

On her eighth birthday Shirley Temple was made an honorary G-Man by J. Edgar Hoover. She was made an honorary captain in the Texas Rangers and an honorary colonel in the American Legion.

For a while there was talk of borrowing Shirley Temple from 20th Century-Fox in exchange for the services of Jean Harlow and Clark Gable at MGM so that Shirley could play Dorothy in *The Wizard of Oz*. Harlow's death in 1937 prevented this arrangement from happening.

Former child actress Shirley Temple has served as U.S. Ambassador to Ghana.

Shirley Temple–Deanna Durbin–Elizabeth Taylor–Tatum O'Neal

Shirley Temple received her first screen kiss from Dickie Moore in *Miss Annie Rooney* (1942). Deanna Durbin was first kissed by Robert Stack in *First Love* (1939). Elizabeth Taylor's first screen kiss was from Marshall Thompson in *Cynthia* (1946). Tatum O'Neal's first screen kiss was from Jeffrey Byron in *International Velvet* (1978).

Shirley Temple–Jane Withers

In 1937 two child actresses were in the top ten of the *Motion Picture Herald*'s survey of moneymaking stars. Shirley Temple was number one and Jane Withers was number three.

The Ten Commandments (1956)

Herb Alpert, now a millionaire record producer and artist, played a drummer in Cecil B. De Mille's 1956 religious spectacular *The Ten Commandments*.

Irving Thalberg

Irving Thalberg became production chief of Universal studios at the age of twenty; later he was an executive at MGM. Tragically, the "boy genius" died at the young age of thirty-seven. F. Scott Fitzgerald patterned his final novel, *The Last Tycoon*, after the life of Thalberg.

The only time that movie producer Irving Thalberg's name appeared on the screen was in a dedication in the credits of the 1937 film *The Good Earth*, his last motion picture.

Phyllis Thaxter

Actress Phyllis Thaxter is the daughter of a Supreme Court justice from Maine.

The Thing–The Gorilla

Everyone should know that James Arness played the title role in *The Thing* (1951), but did you know that Walter Pidgeon played the title role in *The Gorilla* (1927)?

The Thin Man

The Thin Man (1934) does not refer to Nick Charles (William Powell). It referred to the victim of a murder that Charles investigates. The victim's name was Clyde Wynant, played by Edward Ellis.

This Is the Army

In the 1943 movie *This Is the Army*, future Senator George Murphy played the father of future Governor Ronald Reagan.

Danny Thomas

Danny Thomas used to contribute his yearly income of $450,000 for his Maxwell House Coffee commercials and of $150,000 for Norelco advertisements to the St. Jude Children's Hospital.

Frankie Thomas

Actor Frankie Thomas is a bridge master and is the author of the popular book *The Sherlock Holmes Bridge Book.*

Richard Thomas

The parents of actor Richard Thomas, Richard Thomas III, and Barbara (Fallis) Thomas, own the New York School of Ballet.

Fred Thomson

Western actor Fred Thomson was one of the most athletic men ever to go into acting. While attending Occidental College in Los Angeles he broke the record set by Jim Thorpe in the decathlon.

Jim Thorpe

Olympian Jim Thorpe played the captain of the guards in the 1935 movie *She* and a prisoner in the 1949 movie *White Heat.*

Thunder Road

The theme song of the 1958 movie *Thunder Road* was sung and co-composed by Robert Mitchum who starred in the film. Mitchum also produced and wrote the screenplay for this film in which his son Jim made his screen debut. Elvis Presley was originally asked to play the lead role but turned it down.

Times Square

Gene Hackman, Tony Franciosa, Lily Tomlin, and Sandy Duncan all at one time worked at the Howard Johnson restaurant located near Times Square in New York City.

Thelma Todd

Thelma Todd was selected as Miss Massachusetts in her youth. Prior to becoming an actress, she was a school teacher.

Mike Todd

Movie producer Mike Todd was the first American civilian to enter Berlin in 1945, after the fall of Nazi Germany.

Mike Todd–Jack E. Leonard

Avrom Hirsch Goldbogen and Fat Libitsky attended Wicker Park Grammar School together in Chicago. They were good friends and indulged in boyhood pranks a number of times.

Avrom became producer Mike Todd and Fat Libitsky grew up to become comedian Jack E. Leonard.

TOEs

All of the following performers have been awarded a Tony, an Oscar, and an Emmy: Jack Albertson, Ingrid Bergman, Shirley Booth, Melvyn Douglas, Helen Hayes, Liza Minnelli, Thomas Mitchell, Rita Moreno, and Paul Scofield.

Franchot Tone

Franchot Tone played the President of the United States who was dying of cancer in the 1962 movie *Advise and Consent*. Tone, who died in 1968, was a cancer victim.

The Tonight Show

"Johnny's Theme," the music used on *The Tonight Show*, was written by Paul Anka who makes $30,000 a year in royalties from the playing of the song. Anka listed Johnny Carson as the cowriter.

Tony–Trigger–Champion

Three horses have their hoof prints at Grauman's Chinese Theatre. They are Tony, the horse of Tom Mix; Trigger, the horse of Roy Rogers; and Champion, the horse of Gene Autry.

Too Many Parents

In 1936 twenty-one-year-old Frances Farmer made her movie debut in *Too Many Parents*. The film was shown at the Paramount Theater in her hometown of Seattle. It was the same theater at which she had worked as an usherette two years earlier.

Torch Song

In the 1953 movie *Torch Song* Joan Crawford's singing was dubbed by India Adams.

Peter Tork

Ex-Monkee Peter Tork spent four months in Federal prison in 1972 for possession of marijuana.

Rip Torn

Rip Torn left the cast of *Easy Rider* in 1969 and was replaced by Jack Nicholson.

Spencer Tracy

Spencer Tracy's first movie, *Up the River* (1930), was Humphrey Bogart's second movie.

Spencer Tracy's Oscar for the 1937 movie *Captains Courageous* was mistakenly inscribed to "Dick Tracy."

Due to illness Spencer Tracy was replaced by Edward G. Robinson in the role of Lancie Howard in *The Cincinnati Kid* (1965).

Spencer Tracy–Bette Davis

April 5 is the birthday of two Academy Award winners: Spencer Tracy and Bette Davis.

Spencer Tracy–Katharine Hepburn

Spencer Tracy and Katharine Hepburn have been nominated for Academy Awards more times than any other actor or actress. Tracy, nine times and Hepburn, eleven times.

Spencer Tracy–Pat O'Brien

Spencer Tracy and Pat O'Brien were friends from childhood, attending Marquette Academy in Milwaukee and joining the U.S. Navy together in 1918.

Spencer Tracy–Lowell Thomas

How the West Was Won, the 1963 epic narrated by Spencer Tracy, was the first Cinerama *fiction* movie. The first Cinerama movie, *This Is Cinerama* (1952), was narrated by Lowell Thomas.

John Travolta

John Travolta played bit parts on the TV soaps *The Edge of Night* and *The Secret Storm*. He also appeared in over forty-five television commercials.

In July 1978 John Travolta became the

first male to have his picture on the cover of *McCall's* magazine in over one hundred years.

The Treasure of the Sierra Madre

Two father-son combinations appeared in the 1948 movie *The Treasure of the Sierra Madre*. Jack Holt appeared in a crowd scene, while his son Tim played Curtin. Walter Huston played Howard, while his son John played the man in the white hat. John Huston also directed. Walter Huston won an Oscar for Best Supporting Actor. John Huston took home Oscars for Best Director and Best Screenplay.

Leon Trotsky–Fidel Castro

Leon Trotsky appeared as an extra in movies filmed in New Jersey. Fidel Castro was an extra in several Hollywood films.

Tom Tryon

Former actor Tom Tryon has authored several best-selling novels. One of them, *The Other*, was made into a movie in 1972.

Sonny Tufts

In 1944 Sonny Tufts was listed as number one on the *Motion Picture Herald* list of 10 Stars of Tomorrow.

Sonny Tufts–Ginger Rogers

Sonny Tufts and Ginger Rogers shared the same birthdate, July 16, 1911.

Lana Turner

Contrary to the popular story, Lana Turner was not discovered while sitting on a stool at Schwab's Drug Store. Billy Wilkerson, publisher of *Hollywood Reporter*, discovered a girl in Currie's Ice Cream Parlor across from Hollywood High School named Julia Turner, and voilà—Lana Turner.

Lana Turner–Elizabeth Taylor

Lana Turner's film debut was in the 1937 version of *A Star Is Born*, not *They Won't Forget* (1937) as is usually thought. Likewise, Elizabeth Taylor's first film was neither *Lassie Come Home* (1943) nor *National Velvet* (1944) but *There's One Born Every Minute* (1942).

Ben Turpin

Famous silent screen star Ben Turpin had an insurance policy with Lloyds of London for $1,000,000 to protect his famous crossed eyes from becoming normal.

TWA Flight 94

On November 18, 1950, TWA Flight 94, a constellation flying from Los Angeles to Chicago, lost two (out of four) engines after take-off and was forced to land at Long Beach where it immediately lost a third engine after crashing through a fence. No one on the plane was injured, including passengers John Ford,

Ward Bond, Nancy Olson, and Elizabeth Taylor.

Twins

Because of strict laws protecting child actors, twins are often used to portray young children. At one time Richard Lee and Ronald Lee Simmons played Little Ricky on *I Love Lucy*. Later, twins Michael and Joseph Mayer played the part. David and Stephen Born played Christopher Hapgood Day on the series *Happy*. Erin and Diane Murphy played Tabitha Stevens on *Bewitched*. Rachell Lindsay and Robin Sidney Greenbush played Carrie Ingalls on *Little House on the Prairie*. Justin and Jason Draeger played Joey Stivic on *All in the Family*.

Tom Tyler

Actor Tom Tyler once held the world's heavyweight weight-lifting championship for fourteen years. He also had broken six records when he competed in the Olympics. He appeared in several classics including *Gone With The Wind* (1939), *Stagecoach* (1939), *The Westerner* (1940), and *She Wore a Yellow Ribbon* (1949).

U

Leslie Uggams

As a young girl Leslie Uggams won $25,000 on the TV game show *Name That Tune*. She made a return visit and again won $25,000. She was a regularly featured singer on the NBC TV show *Sing Along with Mitch*.

The Ugly American

Kukrit Pramoj, who played the premier of the fictitious country of Sarkhan in the 1962 movie *The Ugly American*, actually became the premier of Thailand in 1974.

Union Pacific

The very same golden spike that was used to link the Union Pacific and Central Pacific railroads at Promontory Point, Utah, on May 10, 1869 was used in the Cecil B. De Mille movie *Union Pacific* (1939), which reenacted the incident.

United Artists

In 1919 Douglas Fairbanks, Mary Pickford, Charles Chaplin, and D. W. Griffith formed United Artists. The first United Artists release was *His Majesty the American* (1919). Boris Karloff appeared in the film as an extra.

U.S. Delegates to the United Nations

Shirley Temple, Irene Dunne, Pearl Bailey, Marian Anderson, and Paul Newman have all served as U.S. delegates to the United Nations.

Peter Ustinov

As an enlisted man in the British Army during World War II Peter Ustinov served as Lt. Colonel David Niven's batman (orderly).

Among Peter Ustinov's many awards is the Order of the Smile for his assistance to the World's Children Organization. It was presented to him in Warsaw in 1974.

V

Karen Valentine

Karen Valentine was a contestant in the Miss Teenage America Contest and was awarded the title of Miss Talent U.S.A.

Valentino

Rodolpho Alfonzo Raffaele Pierre Filibert Guglielmi di Valentino d'Antonguolla was the full name of silent film star Rudolph Valentino.

Rudy Vallee

The first singing telegram was delivered on July 28, 1933, to Rudy Vallee. The delivery boy sang "Happy Birthday."

Valley of the Dolls

Susan Hayward's singing voice was dubbed by Margaret Whiting in the 1967 movie *Valley of the Dolls*.

Robert Vaughn

As a young lad Robert Vaughn played Billy Fairfield on the radio series *Jack Armstrong —The All American Boy* for a short time. Vaughn's father, Gerald Walter Vaughn, appeared as a regular on the radio shows *Crime Doctor* and *Gangbusters*.

Robert Vaughn received a Ph.D. in communications. His dissertation concerned the Hollywood Ten and the blacklisting of the early 1950s. The title of his work is *Only Victims* (1972).

Herve Villechaize

Three foot, eleven inch tall French-born actor Herve Villechaize claims to have psychic powers.

Viva Knievel

For his 1977 biographical movie *Viva Knievel*, famous motorcycle stunt jumper Robert Craig "Evel" Knievel had a double in the film named Gary Davis to perform the more difficult stunts.

Voices

Three television producers have done off-camera voices for their shows. William Dozier was the narrator for *Batman*. Lorenzo Music was the voice of Carlton the Doorman on *Rhoda*. James Komack provided the voice of principal John Lazarus on *Welcome Back, Kotter*.

Erich Von Stroheim

Famed director Erich Von Stroheim served in the Austrian cavalry and spent two years in the U.S. Cavalry. He also served in the Mexican Army against Pancho Villa.

Harry Von Zell

Harry Von Zell, who at one time was a singer with Charlie Barnet's band, committed one of the greatest bloopers of all time when he introduced the President of the United States by saying "Ladies and gentlemen, the President of the United States, Hoovert Heever."

W

Lyle Waggoner

In 1976 actor Lyle Waggoner was elected mayor of Encino, California.

Lindsay Wagner

At the age of ten *Bionic Woman* star Lindsay Wagner was the baby sitter for Glen Campbell's children.

Robert Wagner

As a young man Robert Wagner cut a record titled "Almost Eighteen."

Robert Wagner–Natalie Wood

Robert Wagner and Natalie Wood not only believed that they were meant for each other once but went to the altar twice (1957 and 1972).

Wagon Train

In an episode of the TV series *Wagon Train* aired on November 23, 1960, John Wayne played General Sherman in a cameo role that was directed by John Ford. In the credits he was billed as Michael Morrison. He again played General Sherman in *How the West Was Won* (1963).

Clint Walker

Valerie Petrie, one of the few female airline pilots in the United States, is the daughter of actor Clint Walker.

Robert Walker

After Robert Walker's divorce from actress Jennifer Jones, he married Barbara Ford, the daughter of director John Ford. The marriage lasted only a week.

Mike Wallace

News commentator Mike Wallace was at one time the announcer for the TV series *Sky King*.

Raoul Walsh

Director Raoul Walsh's brother, George Walsh, played an escaped convict in the 1932 movie *Me and My Gal.*

Walter Wanger

American independent movie producer Walter Wanger, responsible for such movies as *Stagecoach* (1939) and *Foreign Correspondent* (1940), was arrested and sent to prison for shooting Jennings Lang, the agent of his wife, actress Joan Bennett. After his release he produced several anti-prison pictures such as *Riot in Cell Block 11* (1954) and *I Want To Live!* (1958).

In 1948 Walter Wanger turned down a Special Academy Award presented to him as producer of the movie *Joan of Arc.*

Jack Warden

In his youth Jack Warden fought as a welterweight under the ring name of Johnny Costello.

Doris Warner

Doris Warner, the daughter of movie producer Harry Warner, has been married to Mervyn LeRoy, Charles Vidor, and Billy Rose.

Sam Warner

Sam Warner, one of the four founders of Warner Bros. Pictures and a proponent of talk-

ing movies, passed away the day before Warner Bros. released the first talkie, *The Jazz
Singer*, with Al Jolson. Warner died on October
5, 1927.

War of the Worlds

The Flying Wing bomber used to drop an
A-bomb on the Martians in the 1953 sci-fi movie *War of the Worlds* is the same aircraft that is
today the only remaining Flying Wing in exis-
tence. It is kept at the Smithsonian Institution.

Jennifer Warren

In her first four movie appearances actress
Jennifer Warren played opposite Paul New-
man, Robert De Niro, Gene Hackman, and
James Caan.

Ethel Waters

In 1942 Ethel Waters was made an honorary captain in the California State Militia.

John Wayne

Although many film buffs know John
Wayne by the name Marion Michael Morrison,
his name is listed as Marion Robert Morrison
on his birth certificate.

John Wayne was given the nickname
Duke because of a pet Airedale named Duke
which he had as a young boy.

John Wayne was president of his senior class at Glendale High School. He also won the Southern California Shakespeare Oratory Contest in his senior year.

Two of John Wayne's wives were the daughters of politicians. Josephine Saenz (1933) was the daughter of the Panamanian Consul in Los Angeles. Pilar Palette (1954) was the daughter of a Peruvian senator.

John Wayne was paid $500,000 for making a Datril commercial for TV in 1977.

John Wayne movies have grossed over $400,000,000—more money than any other performer's films.

Carl Weathers

Carl Weathers, who played Apollo Creed in the *Rocky* movies, previously played football with the Oakland Raiders.

Dennis Weaver

In 1948 Dennis Weaver was a runner-up for the decathlon in the U.S. Olympic trials.

Clifton Webb

Clifton Webb, whose real name was Webb Parmalee Hollenbeck, sang in an opera in Boston at the age of seventeen.

Clifton Webb did not make his motion picture debut in the 1944 movie *Laura* as is usually supposed. He appeared earlier in at least three silent movies: *Polly with a Past*

(1921), *New Toys* (1925), and *The Heart of Siren* (1925).

Jack Webb

Brant Parker, the man who created *The Wizard of Id*, attended the same high school as Jack Webb, who was then student body president. Webb was the cartoonist for the school paper. Parker had not yet gone into cartooning, nor Webb into acting.

Richard Webb

Richard Webb, who played *Captain Midnight* on television, was in reality a lieutenant colonel in the U.S. Army Reserves.

Johnny Weissmuller

When Johnny Weissmuller was given the part of Tarzan he was under contract to BVD (Bradley, Voorhees, Day) to model underwear and swimming trunks. MGM had to agree to have stars like Jean Harlow, Greta Garbo, Joan Crawford, and Marie Dressler model BVD swimwear in order to get Weissmuller for the role.

Raquel Welch

Raquel Welch was once Miss San Diego. After high school graduation she worked as a weather girl on a San Diego TV station.

Robert L. Welch

The son of movie producer Robert L. Welch, Bob Welch, is a former member of the highly popular rock group Fleetwood Mac.

Tuesday Weld

Susan is Tuesday Weld's real first name, and she was actually born on Thursday, August 27, 1943.

Tuesday Weld turned down starring leads in such movies as *Bonnie and Clyde* (1967), *Cactus Flower* (1969), *Bob & Carol and Ted & Alice* (1969), and *True Grit* (1969).

Harold Wellman

Harold Wellman was an assistant cameraman during the filming of *King Kong* in 1933. Forty-three years later Wellman was a special effects cameraman for the second version of *King Kong* (1976).

William Wellman

Director William Wellman saw plenty of action in World War I. After serving for a short time in the U.S. Ambulance Corps, he enlisted in the French Foreign Legion. From there he entered the Lafayette Flying Corps (Escadrille No. 87) and ended his military career with the U.S. Aviation Service. France awarded him the Croix de Guerre for his service. Wellman directed such classics as *The Public Enemy*

(1931), *Beau Geste* (1939), and *The Ox-Bow Incident* (1943).

Mae West

In 1926 Mae West appeared in a play that she also wrote and produced. Its title was *Sex*. The New York police raided the theater, and Miss West was found guilty of obscenity. She was fined $500 and sentenced to ten days on Welfare Island. She received two days off for good behavior.

"Mae West" was the name given to inflatable life jackets by the British RAF during World War II and is today recognized by lexicographers (compilers of dictionaries).

The Westerner

Dana Andrews and Forrest Tucker made their motion picture debuts in the same 1940 movie, *The Westerner*.

James Whale

Director James Whale became interested in show business while he was a prisoner of war in a German stalag in World War I. He put on numerous camp shows.

When the Daltons Rode

When the Daltons Rode (1940), which starred Randolph Scott, was based on a book of the same title by Emmett Dalton, a member of the famed Dalton Brothers gang and a survivor of the Coffeyville, Kansas, raid (October 5, 1892). Emmett produced a silent film about the Dalton gang titled *Beyond the Law,* in which he portrayed himself.

Stuart Whitman

Actor Stuart Whitman was a light-heavyweight boxer during his service in the U.S. Army.

James Whitmore

James Whitmore was once a member of Yale University's singing society, the Whiffenpoofs.

Richard Widmark

In his senior year at his Princeton, Illinois High School Richard Widmark served as class president.

Richard Widmark, an actor in many war movies, was rejected by the U.S. Army in World War II because of a perforated eardrum.

The Wild Bunch

In the 1969 movie *The Wild Bunch* more blank ammunition was fired in the making of the film than real ammunition was fired in the entire Mexican Revolution.

Cornel Wilde

Muscular actor Cornel Wilde has brains as well as brawn. He graduated from Townsend Harris High School in New York at the age of fourteen.

Cornel Wilde was such an avid fencer that he was selected to join the U.S. team for the 1936 Olympics held in Berlin. He did not attend for personal reasons.

The Wild One

The 1954 movie *The Wild One* was based on an actual incident which occurred on July 4, 1947, in the small California town of Hollister when a motorcycle gang terrorized the town.

The British censor board was so shocked by *The Wild One* that it was not shown in England until twelve years after the movie was released.

Ashley Wilkes

Melvyn Douglas, Ray Milland, Robert Young, and Lew Ayres were all considered for the part of Ashley Wilkes in *Gone With The Wind*. The Southern gentleman was played by Englishman Leslie Howard.

Andy Williams

Singer Andy Williams at age fourteen provided some of the singing for Lauren Bacall in her movie debut, *To Have and Have Not* (1944).

Bill Williams

Actor Bill Williams, aside from having been both a professional dancer and actor, was the Junior Scholastic Swimming Champion in 1934 and 1935 in both the 220- and 440-meter races.

Guinn "Big Boy" Williams

Guinn Williams, son of U.S. Congressman Guinn Williams, Sr., was himself elected to Congress representing Texas.

Humorist Will Rogers gave Guinn Williams his nickname of "Big Boy" while working with him on a movie.

Roy Williams

Big Mouseketeer Roy Williams designed the insignia for the Flying Tigers and the Navy Seabees.

Tennessee Williams

Thomas Lanier Williams, better known as Tennessee Williams, wrote his Pulitzer Prize-winning play, *A Streetcar Named Desire*, for Tallulah Bankhead, his choice for the part of Blanche DuBois.

William Tell

If Errol Flynn had had proper financial backing his uncompleted 1953 movie *William Tell* would have made history as the first movie filmed in CinemaScope. Thirty minutes of the picture was completed before the work was abandoned.

Chill Wills

Chill Wills was given his humorous first name by his parents because he was born on the hottest day in the town's history which was July 18, 1903 in Seagoville, Texas.

Chill Wills provided the singing voice for actor Ken Farrell in the 1947 movie *Heartaches*.

Dooley Wilson

Dooley Wilson's piano-playing was performed by Elliott Carpenter in *Casablanca*. Wilson was also seen as a piano player in *Higher and Higher* (1943). In reality Wilson could not play the piano.

Henry Wilson

Henry Wilson was the man responsible for renaming Marilyn Louis (Rhonda Fleming), Arthur Gelien (Tab Hunter), Merle Johnson (Troy Donahue), and Elmore Torn (Rip Torn).

Paul Winchell

Ventriloquist Paul Winchell was granted a patent for his blood transferral apparatus, and he has also invented an artificial heart.

Walter Winchell

Walter Winchell received $25,000 per episode to narrate the Desilu television series *The Untouchables*.

Winchester '73

Future superstars Rock Hudson and Tony Curtis both had bit parts in the 1950 movie *Winchester '73*. Hudson played an Indian, Curtis a soldier.

Wings

Wings (1927), the first movie to win an Academy Award for Best Picture, was also the only silent film to win such an award. Gary Cooper appeared in a minor role in the film.

Henry Winkler

Henry Winkler's first Broadway play, *42 Seconds from Broadway*, closed the same night that it opened.

Henry Winkler, who has played a high school dropout in both the 1974 movie *The Lords of Flatbush* and the TV series *Happy Days*, has a master's degree in dramatic arts from Yale.

Shelley Winters

While in high school Shelley Winters was editor of her Thomas Jefferson High School newspaper.

Shelley Winters's Oscar for Best Supporting Actress in 1959's *The Diary of Anne Frank* is kept in Amsterdam at the Anne Frank Museum (the very same building in which Anne hid for twenty-five months).

Grant Withers

Grant Withers married Loretta Young in 1930. In 1931 the couple made the film *Too Young To Marry*. Shortly after the movie's completion they were divorced.

The Wizard of Oz

In 1939 the *Harvard Lampoon* called *The Wizard of Oz* a most colossal flop.

The Women

George Cukor directed *The Women* (1939). The cast consisted of 135 actresses; among them were Joan Crawford, Paulette Goddard, and Norma Shearer. No males appeared in the film.

Wonder Woman

The recent upsurge in comic book heroes and heroines, especially *Wonder Woman* (played on TV by Lynda Carter), is something for a psychologist to ponder. It was psychologist William Moulton Marston who created *Wonder Woman*, which he introduced in 1941. He was a lawyer as well, and as a matter of fact, was the inventor of the polygraph (lie detector) in 1915.

Natalie Wood

Natalie Wood, born Natasha Gurdin, was given her screen name by movie executives William Goetz and Leo Spitz in honor of their late friend, director Sam Wood.

As a young girl Natalie Wood spent a year on the TV series *Pride of the Family* (broadcast from 1953 to 1954). Fay Wray also appeared on the program.

Natalie Wood–Diana Rigg

Natalie Wood and Diana Rigg were both born on July 20, 1938.

Woody Woodpecker

Because of the great friendship between special-effects expert George Pal and animator Walter Lantz, many of Pal's films have an appearance by Woody Woodpecker, Lantz's creation.

Monty Woolley

Monty Woolley served in the Mexican Border campaign and in World War I. He returned to Yale as an instructor of dramatic writing, where among his students were Thornton Wilder and Stephen Vincent Benét.

Monty Woolley was president of the Yale

Dramatic Association when Cole Porter attended the University. In the 1946 film *Night and Day* Woolley portrayed himself teaching Cole Porter (Cary Grant) at Yale.

Teresa Wright

Teresa Wright was nominated in two categories for her 1942 film work. She received a nomination for Best Actress for *Pride of the Yankees* (as Mrs. Lou Gehrig) and a nomination for Best Supporting Actress for her role of Carol Beldon for *Mrs. Miniver.* She won for the latter performance.

Jane Wyatt

Jane Wyatt is a descendant, on her father's side, of Philip Livingston, a signer of the Declaration of Independence. On her mother's side she is descended from Rufus King, founder of Columbia University.

Keenan Wynn

Keenan Wynn has ridden a motorcycle into a car. He destroyed a speed boat as he crashed into a pile of rocks at 60 m.p.h. He has totaled at least four cars, including a Jaguar and a Porsche. He has survived two plane crashes and once raced motorcycles in the desert at speeds over 150 m.p.h.

Keenan Wynn is the uncle of the Hudson Brothers: Mark, Brett, and Bill.

Tracy Keenan Wynn

Tracy Keenan Wynn, son of Keenan Wynn and grandson of Ed Wynn, wrote the screenplays for *The Longest Yard* (1974), *The Autobiography of Miss Jane Pittman* (1974), and *The Deep* (1977).

Y

Yankee Doodle Dandy

Al Jolson bought the first ticket to George M. Cohan's play *Yankee Doodle Dandy* at a cost of $25,000. The proceeds of the ticket sale went to charity.

The Yearling

The Yearling was originally planned as a project involving Spencer Tracy, Anne Revere, and Gene Eckman. These actors were replaced by Gregory Peck, Jane Wyman, and Claude Jarman, Jr., for the 1946 movie.

Gig Young

Byron Barr, better known as Gig Young,

took his stage name from a character he played in the 1945 film *The Gay Sisters*.

Loretta Young

Loretta Young and her sisters appeared as extras in the 1926 Valentino movie *Son of the Shiek* as Arab girls.

The American Institute of Voice Teachers named Loretta Young as possessing the best feminine speaking voice for four years in a row.

Victor Young

Peter Finch was not the first person to be awarded an Oscar posthumously. Victor Young, who died on November 11, 1956, was voted an Oscar in 1957 for his work on *Around the World in Eighty Days* for Best Score of a Dramatic or Comedy Picture.

Your Cheatin' Heart

In the 1964 biographical movie *Your Cheatin' Heart*, Hank Williams, Jr. dubbed in the singing voice of his father for actor George Hamilton.

You're in the Navy Now

Charles Bronson and Lee Marvin both debuted in the same movie, *You're in the Navy Now* (1951).

Z

Darryl F. Zanuck

While in the U.S. Army Darryl F. Zanuck learned to box. He was in twenty-six bantam-weight bouts.

Darryl F. Zanuck, a recipient of the Legion of Merit, began in Hollywood as a writer of Rin Tin Tin movies.

Darryl F. Zanuck considered 13 his lucky number. He always owned a car with a 13 somewhere on the license plate. He even went so far as to change the title of the 1946 movie *32 Rue Madeleine* to *13 Rue Madeleine*. The name Darryl F. Zanuck has 13 letters, of course. However, he smoked an average of 20 cigars a day.

Efrem Zimbalist, Jr.

Efrem Zimbalist, Jr., is the son of concert violinist Efrem Zimbalist and opera singer Alma Gluck.

Efrem Zimbalist, Jr., is the co-producer of three operas and is the composer of classical music that has been performed.

Vera Zorina

Vera Zorina was to play Maria in the 1943 film *For Whom the Bell Tolls*, but she was replaced by Ingrid Bergman. Miss Zorina threatened to sue Paramount, so they gave her a cash settlement.

Adolf Zukor

At movie producer Adolf Zukor's 100th birthday party, Paramount Pictures auctioned off the candles on his cake for $1,000 apiece. The money went to charity.

... and finally, here's to Zasu Pitts who never:

boxed in college
won a medal in the Olympics
turned down *High Sierra*
invented anything
won a Grammy, a Tony, an Emmy, or an Oscar ... but we love you just the same!